Right Now Enough Is Enough!

Overcoming Your Addictions and Bad Habits For Good...

Peter Andrew Sacco PH.D.

DISCLAIMER

This book details the author's personal experiences with and opinions about addictions. The author is not a healthcare provider.

The author and publisher are providing this book and its contents on an "as is" basis and make no representations or warranties of any kind with respect to this book or its contents. The author and publisher disclaim all such representations and warranties, including for example warranties of merchantability and healthcare for a particular purpose. In addition, the author and publisher do not represent or warrant that the information accessible via this book is accurate, complete or current.

The statements made about products and services have not been evaluated by the U.S. Food and Drug Administration. They are not intended to diagnose, treat, cure, or prevent any condition or disease. Please consult with your own physician or healthcare specialist regarding the suggestions and recommendations made in this book.

Except as specifically stated in this book, neither the author or publisher, nor any authors, contributors, or other representatives will be liable for damages arising out of or in connection with the use of this book. This is a comprehensive limitation of liability that applies to all damages of any kind, including (without limitation) compensatory; direct, indirect or consequential damages; loss of data, income or profit; loss of or damage to property and claims of third parties.

You understand that this book is not intended as a substitute for consultation with a licensed healthcare practitioner, such as your physician. Before you begin any healthcare program, or change your lifestyle in any way, you will consult your physician or other licensed healthcare practitioner to ensure that you are in good health and that the examples contained in this book will not harm you.

This book provides content related to topics physical and/or mental health issues. As such, use of this book implies your acceptance of this disclaimer.

PRAISE FOR RIGHT NOW ENOUGH IS ENOUGH!

William D. (in recovery A.A.): "An absolute must read for anyone with an addiction or really bad habit. Also, great if you are in Al-Anon or have a family or friend coping with an addiction. This book really works! It is the first of its kind to offer hope for anyone with addiction by covering every possible way for recovery instead of focusing on just one approach and shunning people away!"

Lauren R. (self-help advocate/in recovery A.A.) :This book will change your life for the better instantly! I have worked 'the program' as well as others and this puts things in perspective immediately. Dr. Peter Sacco understands it, gets it and applies it for people with addictions to use and fix themselves instantly. You will never be the same once you read this book and use it to overcoming addiction."

Sanderson Layng (Vice President and Chief Operating Officer Canadian Centre for Abuse Awareness): "Addressing any addiction successfully requires 2 key elements - first you have to make the commitment to change and then you have to consistently change your patterns of behaviour until you kick it. In this book, Dr. Sacco helps you do both by challenging you to make that commitment and then giving you a range of tools that can help you be successful."

DEDICATION

This book is dedicated to all the people I have worked with over the years--colleagues, clients, friends, participants at workshops and readers. You have taught me so much over the last two decades and provided me with the ideals to create a treatment program for addiction that truly works!

TABLE OF CONTENTS

FOREWARD

I have known Peter for many years now. I have had the privilege of sitting in on his lectures as well as having him work with me one on one in session. When you have bad habits or addictions, as is my case, you really struggle to find something that works to help you not only kick the vice, but also remain clean. Most types and methods of therapies and treatments for addictions are so one-sided that if you don't buy into the complete process, then getting complete as a person is hard to process!

Peter let me read this book as he was working on it. He also allowed me to add my input into his ideas, not that he needed them as he was on the right track. He created something in this book that is applicable to anyone or everyone who possesses an addiction, or a bad habit. Also, if you just want to improve yourself or your attitude, then this book will be of help to you.

If you apply the principles and methods used in this book you will notice positive results. You may or will not get them overnight, but you will get them if you stay the course!

I strongly recommend this book to everyone/anyone with an addiction or a bad habit. I also recommend reading it if you have a loved one with an addiction whom you are supporting. This book will help you understand addictions/habits at many levels, some I never knew even existed! You will also learn about how your past and the negative stuff you hold onto makes you so bitter that you are where you are today..miserable. The flipside is you will learn about sweet acceptance in this book, that "ah ha" moment when you "finally get it"! You will overcome whatever it is you want to release in your life and get what you want...peace of mind!

Thank you Peter for writing this book filled with knowledge, ideas and methods for optimal living. You really put it all together in one book! Peace!

William D.

INTRODUCTION:

LIVING A LIFE BASED ON EXPECTATION – YOUR OWN!

"Life is largely a matter of expectation."

Horace

The "spiritual model" has been widely employed in twelve-step programmes throughout the world for the treatment of addictions. Many alcoholics find great help from a Divine Power with groups and sponsors when they work in programmes such as Alcoholics Anonymous. The "Big Book", used by A.A. groups, brings many individuals to a place they are not too familiar with: Spiritualism.

As technology has produced new and insightful means through which to cope with addictions, nothing can supersede the positive effect of the twelve-step programme. It seems there is nothing greater than the root of the twelve-step programme itself: surrendering to a Higher Power. If someone has problems with their automobile, they take it back to the manufacturer who created it so it can get fixed. God is the manufacturer of human beings, therefore, the same premise should hold true. If we humans need fixing, then why not call upon our manufacturer to fix us? There are some who like to refer to "God" or their creator as the "Universe" or "Divine Mind". Whatever works best for those calling upon that name, only they know! Whether you are a believer or not, there are some laws that permeate the universe we live in – gravity, cause and effect, aging, etc. There is also a Law of Attraction which exists. When you think, feel and then act a certain way, you will create certain results for yourself. Furthermore, these results are consistent! When you act in a positive way you usually invoke positive outcomes, and when you act and think negatively, you get negative results. If you don't believe, give it a try for a week at your own risk! I don't encourage trying this simple test, because you won't like the results. The unfortunate part is people live this way on a daily basis, either by their own choosing, or by proxy. When I refer to "by proxy", they have been negative for so long that negativity becomes second nature to them. In essence, they know of no other way. Furthermore, many who then become of another way of thinking, feeling and acting, are simply too lazy to work on change – a change which could and would have profound and immediate positive effects on their lives!

This book can be used by believers in Jesus Christ/God/the Universe/a Higher Power, people who subscribe to the Law of Attraction/intention or by non-believers. This book contains effective and proven principles for overcoming obstacles in life – addictions, bad habits, negative thinking and anxiety/anger issues. I strongly encourage you to work through this book and see the tremendous results the information will have on your life if you apply it. The principles/methods work...period! They have been used by countless individuals (patients, clients, consumers and colleagues) that I have encountered over the years, both professionally and as acquaintances. Whatever you are doing in your life currently is probably not working, right? If it was, you would probably not be looking for something new to help "fix you" or help you change some undesirable aspect of your life. You have come to the right place.

When you get to the core issues I provide and apply them to your daily living, you are further ahead in life. They hold amazing psychological applications and power of intentions to have, be and create the life you most want. You don't have to believe in a Higher Power for them to work. You first have to believe in yourself, have faith in your abilities, and then take the first step with me in believing for positive change in your life.

When I started writing this book, I consulted with many professionals, colleagues, friends and individuals in recovery. I wanted to create a self-help book that would be user-friendly to anyone who picked it up. Honestly, this book has taken me eight years to complete because of all the experience I needed to learn about, witness, explore and expand upon. Eight years later, this is what I came up with, which has proven TRIED, TESTED and TRUE!

I was asked by members of the media as well as professionals, "How would you best describe the tone/theme of this book?" To paraphrase this, they wanted to know exactly, what methods of operation went into this book, what readers would get out of this book, and what principles they could apply to their lives. I summed it up by combining three components:

4

PSYCHO-SOCIO-SPIRITUAL. There is something for everyone, but if you believe in all three components and live your life accordingly, you will find optimal results. What is the PSYCHO-SOCIO-SPIRITUAL approach I use? Basically, it is a combination of these three elements:

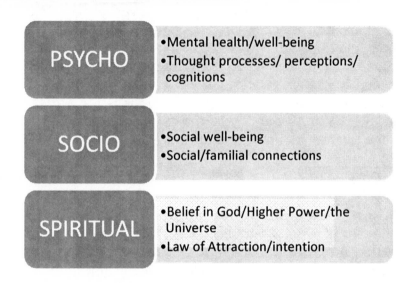

PSYCHO
- Mental health/well-being
- Thought processes/ perceptions/ cognitions

SOCIO
- Social well-being
- Social/familial connections

SPIRITUAL
- Belief in God/Higher Power/the Universe
- Law of Attraction/intention

You are who you are based on what you believe. Healthy thoughts and perceptions will lead you to developing a healthy mind and attitude. They say birds of a feather flock together. Who you choose to associate with, or who you allow into your life says a lot about who you are. Everyone is so much more than what you see on the outside. We are all born with spirit. We are all connected to a Higher Power...God/the Universal Mind! Everyone has the ability to exercise their will in the Universe and draw to them the lives they most want. In this book, I will show you how all three work independently, as well as how they become dependent upon one another. I will give you all of the key components to become who you want to be, have what you want to have and find the path you were most created to walk on – enjoying a journey for everyday living!

With this book, you can take it all, or take just the parts you need depending on where you are psychologically, socially and spiritually. If you are all three, then welcome to the buffet of options...you get everything on the menu!

This book is not only for the "believer" or for "spiritual" people. I will also discuss CBT (Cognitive Behavioral Therapy) and how it is applicable for overcoming and treating habits and addiction. Anyone looking to overcome addictions, bad habits, or wanting to create new habits will benefit from this book. As one member of the media put it, "This book is a great self-help manual for turning your life in the direction you want to go!" Enjoy the journey to a new and greater you!

ABOUT THIS BOOK: The book is broken into 3 sections. In the first part I will discuss the components of what an addiction is, why it continues to exist and fester, and how to overcome addictions and bad habits. In the second section I will discuss the individual compontial causes of addiction/habits and give you the tools to begin overcoming them immediately to place you on your road to recovery fast! Finally, in the third section, you will find 30 days of intentions. Work these into your life for the next thirty days then repeat them for another 30 days.

SECTION ONE

ADDICTION, BITTERNESS AND ACCEPTANCE

CHAPTER ONE:

WHAT IS THE DIFFERENCE BETWEEN ADDICTION AND HABIT?

"It is hard to understand addiction unless you have experienced it."

Ken Hensley

An addiction is a very complex, powerful, and progressive process which renders the individual with the illness helpless and out of control. For many, the first time they used their substance of choice, they became instantly hooked. In fact, most didn't stand a chance.

BIO-PSYCHO-SOCIAL MODEL

Many counselors in the field of addictions today like to look at addictions from a holistic approach. This means they like to treat the problem using a "bio-psycho-social" model. Rather than looking at the individual from one frame of reference, i.e., as only being "biological" creatures, existing only in the "psychological" domain, or being totally "social" beings, where they respond only because they mimic what society influences them to do, they like to look at all three aspects of the individual's being.

The biological aspect deals primarily with the individual's physical body plus the physical make-up of the substance of choice. For example, biologists may assert that certain individuals become addicted because they possess certain genes, have chemical imbalances in the brain, or are physically ill, which makes them predisposed to becoming addicted to certain substances. Furthermore, a stronger case could be made for individuals who were born to alcoholic mothers, who drank before and during pregnancy, mothers who used crack-cocaine and other substances, who increased the likelihood the substance would be in their child's system even before they were born. Cases have emphasized fetal alcohol babies, who are born "intoxicated" or with alcohol on their breath, and "crack" babies who are already "stoned" the minute they come out of the womb. In similar instances, babies are likely to suffer withdrawal symptoms (delirium tremens) if they don't get the substance they are on! Today, more and more research is asserting there is definitely a gene for alcoholism.

The psychological component of addiction points to defects in one's psyche. The psychological component can be split to reflect one of two ideas: the individual actually possesses a mental health illness, or the individual actively seeks out substances which alter their mood and makes them feel their desired state. There are many individuals in the field of addictions who believe those with addictions suffer from mental health disorders. In fact, many professionals would argue the individual has a "concurrent disorder", meaning not only do they have their addiction, but they also have one or more mental health disorders. This is where the "what came first, chicken or egg" scenario starts! Did the person become addicted because they had a mental health problem and they chose drugs to alleviate the symptoms? Or was it the continual use of a particular substance which eventually altered the brain chemistry and neurotransmitters which led to the mental health disorder? There are books and websites which address this debate. Unfortunately, most of the time, the proper treatment becomes debatable and the client never gets the proper help they need. Many hospitals won't treat the mental health disorder until the client is clean and sober, and many treatment centers won't treat the addiction until the individual gets help with the mental health disorder. The sad part is many of these individuals fall through the cracks and continue using.

The second aspect of the psychological component examines how individuals engage in the use of a substance because they become conditioned to it. The individual with the addiction learns that using the drug will make them feel the way they want to feel and it also allows them an escape from their daily pressures. Many of these individuals also become "addicted" to the process of attaining and using their drug of choice. They literally become conditioned like robots to the process of going out and getting their substance and going through the ritual of using. They get a psychological "high" from preparing to use their substance, which then gives them the physical high! Some individuals become "psychologically" addicted to their drug of choice and feel as if they will go crazy if they don't use.

The third component of the model is the sociological component, which looks at how society affects the individual. The general premise here is most individuals with addictions use alcohol, drugs, etc., because they are deemed socially acceptable. In fact, corporations spend millions of dollars to promote their products through the media. Individuals believe if it's legal, then it must be okay to use. And many deny the harmful effects of the drug. Just think, many really, truly didn't believe smoking was as harmful as it was until the Surgeon General affixed the warning on the boxes. Furthermore, many pregnant women drank alcohol and used drugs believing it was okay!

Perhaps one of the most addictive populations in society is teenagers and young adults. Many of them become socialized into using substances because they feel the need to fit in with their peers. The pressure to conform is still paramount for most young people. Being accepted and using drugs creates acceptance and a sense of self-esteem, even at the cost of losing control and becoming addicted!

The best means of treating one's addiction is to encompass all aspects of the individual's being, bio-psycho-social, so no area is left out. By focusing on all areas, you provide the best optimal treatment plan and focus on the individual as a symmetrical being. Spiritualism is becoming more widely accepted in the helping profession and is being seen as a greater influence in the world of addictions than was otherwise given credit for in the past. As the bridged gap between science and religion draws closer, those in the helping profession are recognizing the influence of spiritualism in the healing process.

In the past, any discussion of "spiritualism", when associated with the mental health profession, was viewed as quackery and stupidity. As spiritual twelve-step groups continue to show success with clients, the more the spiritual model is becoming embraced. It is, perhaps, the glue which holds the bio-psycho-social model together. In chapter two, I will discuss in greater detail how the spiritual model effects addiction.

Often times, I have been asked, can someone become addicted to anything? Can anything become addictive? And my answer to that is yes! Depending on one's personality, the circumstances in their life, the network of social influences, their physical and mental health, their need for instant gratification and escapism, anything can become habitual and eventually addictive to fill the void. As an addictions professor and helper, here is a list of the most common substances and behaviors I see individuals battling:

~ alcohol
~ illegal drugs
~ prescription/over the counter drugs
~ gambling
~ tobacco/smoking
~ sports
~ television viewing
~ pornography
~ sex
~ eating
~ anger
~ lying
~ caffeine (coffee/tea)
~ chocolate
~ work
~ Internet
~ religion
~ sleep

That's a pretty long list! I am sure most, if not all of us, engage in some of the activities on the list in healthy moderation. It's when individuals start to cross the line and lose control of their use, and the behavior controls them, that real problems begin to occur.

HABIT VERSUS ADDICTION

What is the difference between a habit and an addiction? Perhaps the best way to answer this question is one word: control. When an individual has a habit, they still have control

over the substance or behavior they are engaging in. They don't think about the habit 24/7, all day and all week. They can use or engage in their activity in moderation. The opposite holds true for an addiction. The substance or behavior controls the user and they can't stop thinking about their next fix. Here is a continuum for the anatomy of an addiction. Notice how the seeds of the addiction are planted and how they continue to flourish along the continuum.

Catharsis/desensitization

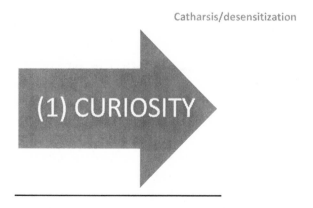

Everything must start with a beginning. There must be a first use. You can't develop an interest in something unless you like it. And you can't like something unless you try it at least once to see if you want to try it again. If you try something for the first time and it produces favorable results, you are more likely to try similar experiences again and move onto stage (2) DESIRE. If the first time experience was really bad, you are less likely to try it again! I know my first time experience with chewing tobacco was horrible. I thought it must taste good if my heroes, pro baseball players, were chewing it. My one encounter with chewing tobacco ranks up there in my most disgusting experiences, and I have never tried it again!

(2) DESIRE

If your first or second experience with curiosity was good, you will more than likely desire to engage in that specific activity again. Desire is sort of like being bitten by an insect suddenly and you start to itch. In this case, you "itch" for the substance which made you feel good. Have you ever watched television, and a commercial break airs an ice cream product and all of a sudden, you get a hankering for a hot fudge sundae? That is the proverbial itch you feel. You desire whatever it is you desire randomly. Not a lot of thought is put into getting your fix of the substance. When desire becomes more frequent and the intensity of it increases, you are then led to what I call the (3) WANT stage.

(3) WANT

Want is the stage where you actually begin to behave in ways which will allow you to engage in the behavior or use your desired substance with more assertion, perhaps even aggressively. It is during this stage where the individual plans ahead with some thought that they are going to get what they "want". Basically, you "want what you want, when you want it!" Desire is more of a hit or miss stimulation. Want is a whole lot stronger and intentional and you are more likely to go out of your way to get what you want. If you see a television commercial at two in the morning for pizza, you may desire pizza but not enough to go out of your way to get one. On the other hand, if you see that same commercial for pizza and you want a pizza, then you will behave more intentionally to secure yourself a pizza. Want is definitely stronger than desire. You can desire something, but not want it. Thank God! If you wanted and got everything desired, divorce rates, etc., would be even higher! When you want something, you definitely desire, which makes the feeling a little more intense. Once we started "wanting" something in particular more and it begins to become part of our regular routine, we are most likely developing to cultivate a (4) HABIT.

(4) HABIT

(4) HABIT

When you arrive at the habit stage, you've reached a point where, often times, you engage in an activity without really giving much thought to it. In fact, it is like your conscious mind is on over-drive and you, more or less, act out of "habit". The activity becomes second nature and you can do it proficiently without paying much attention to it. Perhaps the best example of this is cigarette smoking. When you first start out, you have to pay more attention to lighting the cigarette and playing it properly in your mouth so as not to get burned. Those who have smoked for years have mastered this habit and can light a smoke in the complete dark. Many smokers actually light up first thing in the morning, right after a meal or while driving, without actually even thinking about it. Their unconscious mind usually wants the cigarette and most unconsciously light up without giving it much thought. I often joke in my support groups and with patients in one on one counseling who have come in for hypnosis to try and quit smoking telling them that they have mastered a skill – Smoking! I don't smoke so lighting up is more difficult for me, whereas smokers can light up in the dark. With that said, I assert that if they have mastered the skill of smoking, then they can master the skill of quitting!

The habit component of the road to addiction serves as the gateway to the full-blown, out of control addiction. This is the stage where the wheels literally fall off! Some might refer to it as the point of no return. Two distinct behavioral experiences occur at this point; DESENSITIZATION and CATHARSIS. I will explain what both of these mean.

DESENSITIZATION

Are you a person who likes spicy foods or are you a thrill seeker at amusement parks and enjoy going on fast rides? Do you find that the spicier you make something, it is never hot enough? The more rides you go on, the more intense you crave for them to be, perhaps faster and more adrenaline causing? If you said yes to either, then you have experienced desensitization.

Desensitization can best be described as wanting more of something or a stronger version of it because, over time, you develop a tolerance to it and it doesn't provide the same stimulation. When you eat spicy foods for example, what might have once been considered medium spicy or real spicy were exactly that for your taste buds. Over time you ate so many hot things that both medium and real spicy now seem like mild, and "suicide" spicy seems like real spicy.

The same can be said for speed and rides. Often times what seemed to be very fast in the beginning doesn't seem so fast when you've experienced it enough times. With that said, anything "faster" becomes more stimulating. In a nutshell, you need greater doses or increased helpings to create a satisfying experience which satiates your habit/desire.

CATHARSIS

Do you engage in any activities or situations which help you take the edge off the seriousness of everyday life? Do you find something to do to escape the real world? If whatever you do brings you pleasure, instant gratification and allows you to "escape" then you have engaged in catharsis or a cathartic experience. Catharsis is not a bad thing! In fact, the cathartic experience is a very good one. It keeps us sane and getting caught up in the rigors of living stressful and mundane daily lives. You see, the key to living in harmony or balance is doing things in moderation. It is when the cathartic process becomes the order of the day, doing it too often to escape or be in a state of euphoria/arousal constantly that it no longer is catharsis, but rather a state of being. This state of being is best described as "addiction" to escapism, arousal and/or euphoria. This is when it becomes bad!

DESENSITISATION AND CATHARSIS COMBINED

Now that you know what desensitization and catharsis are, it is time to put them in proper perspective when it comes to explaining when something stops becoming "just a habit" and spills over into becoming "addiction".

When you engage in something repeatedly by choice because it provides you with some sort of pleasure, instant gratification or arousal, then you are in control. You are basically feeding into a habit. You can control the circumstances and how you go about engaging in the experience. Just as fast as you can turn the experience on, you can turn it off and walk away from it. Catharsis is used for escapism or some kind of enjoyment limited in use – moderation. Desensitization has not really occurred as the arousal that the venue or substance is providing is still very good. You are deriving the maximum effects and/or benefits from engaging it. The madness starts when you are using something to escape reality on a daily or regular basis (catharsis) too often and the "escapism" choice is not providing the same arousal or gratification. The key aspect of this experience becomes "NEED"! You have gone past a point of habit or habituation and now engage the daily activity/substance out of necessity. In essence, you believe you "need to do it" to function, perhaps socially in society and maybe even to survive! When need surpasses choice/habit is the point that habit becomes addiction.

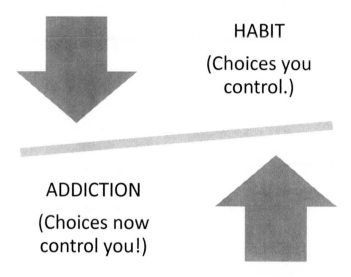

HABIT

(Choices you control.)

ADDICTION

(Choices now control you!)

What you were once able to control by choice (activities providing catharsis) have now become desensitized through overuse/abuse and now you are rendered helpless to them as they have the ability to control you. When something begins to control you and you are helpless to quit it on your own accord, this is when it becomes an addiction. The hallmark of addiction is control – you feel that you have lost control over your life and all areas; physical, psychological, social and spiritual are all out of whack.

(5) NEED

When you hear the term "need" what does it mean to you? What does the word imply when you look at it closely – a sense of desperation, necessity? It implies a lack or "can't do without" mindset. When you examine it in the world of dysfunction pertaining to mental health it is often times equated with co-dependency. In co-dependent relationships (individuals possessing either dependent or independent personality disorders) people "need" people or relationships to give them a sense of identity. They believe they are nothing without their partner. In some ways, their partner is their psychological crutch. When it comes to substance abuse and/or addiction, the user becomes "dependent" on their substance. In much the same way a co-dependent uses another person/relationship as their crutch, the addict does so with a substance.

The longer one starts to believe they "need" something or someone to function or exist is the point where they surrender their freedoms. They believe in a powerful locus of control that exists outside of them which dictates how they should live their life. They believe that states of happiness, peace and contentment can only come from something outside of them. They "need" someone or something to make them feel complete or serve as a diversion for perceived lack of individual completion. Individuals who possess these distorted thought patterns need substances and in some cases people (co-dependent relationships) to satiate them.

Not all needs are bad. Realistically there are certain things people need and can't live without. These would include things like air, water, food, shelter, safety, etc. Abraham Maslow asserted these were necessities along with more abstract things like a sense of belongingness and love, as well as self-esteem to be healthy (Maslow's Hierarchy of Needs). There is a necessity to be in relationships early on in our lives for not only survival but socialization reasons. It is also during this time in secure and healthy families that personal boundaries are taught — knowing where parents, siblings and friends end and you begin. Parents and teachers teach children to live their lives in moderation, helping them to discern how to live life in moderation. When I refer to moderation I mean the subtle as well as complex differences between desires, wants and needs. Being able to distinguish between them, engrain them in thought processes both at conscious and unconscious levels, and using them in the face of freedom (choices) determines where one falls on the continuum of desire versus addiction.

The hallmark of need or necessity is the double-sided coin of frustration/desperation. This is literally the "toss of the coin" which determines the starting point of addiction – the point where "need" ends and addiction begins. By not having one's needs met leads to feelings of stress and eventually frustration. The frustration arises when one perceives they have no control over the situation and tries to get whatever they need to regain control. Desperation goes even further in that that same frustration becomes even more overwhelming and they not only "need" their substance of choice to regain control but they also believe the "substance" is a part of them and without it they are missing a part of themselves. I know this may sound a bit confusing but let me see if I can break this down further.

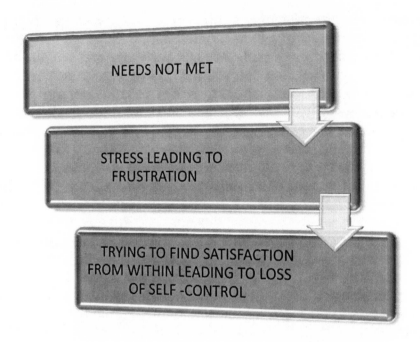

There is a need which means to be fulfilled. Obviously, it is not being met! The longer it goes on without being met the more stress it causes. The individual begins to feel stressed out. As the stress builds, they become even more frustrated. They know they can exert control over this situation if they get whatever it is they need. Even though this need may be irrational, dysfunctional or even damaging in some cases, (i.e. stalking their ex-mate because they "need" them back), they are still able to control the situation on their terms. Even though there may be acts of desperation on their part, they still believe they "hold all the cards". I know this may sound bizarre given the way this individual behaves, but they are still sane in the sense that they know they can control the situation as well as the substance. They discern both how they want the substance to effect them as well as how they want to effect the substance. The hold power over the substance or whatever it is they need, or at least perceived power. They may act desperately in trying to secure whatever it is they need, but this desperation doesn't control them.

This is an interesting point as addicts such as social functioning alcoholics may be put into this aspect of need versus addiction like. Many social functioning alcoholics never appear intoxicated nor do they ever drink to the point of passing out. Some require the "courage from the bottle" to help them get through tasks or situations they find anxiety-provoking. Others drink to take the edge off. They feel they "need" the booze to get them through the moments. Most still believe they are in control of the situation and many are. Perhaps they might be described as practising moderation management before they ever enter a treatment programme, or ever will. And some never will become addicts or aren't addicts! This is where the dichotomy begins and ends with addiction. When an alcoholic drinks "just enough" to function – keeping alcohol in their blood because their body is physiologically addicted to it, or they go into any kind of physical or psychological withdrawal symptoms, then it is an addiction! You see, the need is no longer controlled by them; rather they are controlled by the need. It is totally outside of them and without it, it creates extreme stress and frustration, which produces an insane loss of control. When I refer to "insane" I am referring to the fact that all rationale and logic are tossed by the wayside, as they will do whatever it takes to satisfy their need. You see, their need is bigger than them. Their need is its own entity or persona. It is as if the individual has split in two and a second personality or evil twin has been born. The "evil twin" is their dark-half and they perceive it as being outside of them.

LOSS OF CONTROL

- Intense feelings of desperation.

DESPERATION

- A feeling of lack inside of oneself.

ADDICTION

- Intrinsically trying to overcome feelings of lack.

When this loss of control starts and the dark-half is recognized as being in charge at times or all of the time (the case in full-blown addictions), severe acts of desperation occur. Interestingly, many addicts will assert when they behave badly (either to get their drug of choice or after they have become intoxicated) that it wasn't really them...it was the drug/booze that made them do it. They are not far off in their assessment. It is an alter ego or persona which takes charge or becomes the more dominant force. It's like Bruce Banner (Incredible Hulk) saying, "Don't make me mad...you won't like me when I am mad!" When Banner gets mad he turns green and becomes the Incredible Hulk. When addicts get mad/frustrated they become the color of their addiction! And this is where the madness begins—

Normal functioning people deal rationally and do not behave anti-socially or like sociopaths. I am not saying that addicts possess anti-social personality disorder (DSM-V Axis 2) or are sociopaths, even though some may be. Rather, many who have bad addictions behave in ways that anti-social personality disordered people do. They engage in activities or do things where they no longer feel guilt, shame or remorse. Normal people would feel shame or guilt for stealing. Most would be ashamed of themselves for turning sexual tricks to pay for something. Many would feel dread and remorse for neglecting their families, kids, even jobs to engage in pleasures. However when one behaves desperately more often than they are in control, then feelings of guilt, shame and remorse become superseded by instant gratification and removal of psychological and/or physical pain. The rush and numbing the substance provides removes these feelings. Don't get me wrong as many addicts do feel and think about guilt, shame and remorse, but they are not recognized as being powerful enough or long-lived to get them to stop engaging in substance use. Their dark half rules!

Any perceived control in their lives is believed to come from outside of them. They believe they are lacking/missing something within. They are in a constant state of believing they need to fill this emptiness or void within. They revert to anything and will stop at nothing to fill this void. All rational thought is gone and dysfunctional desperation becomes a daily intention. This is ADDICTION!

CAN'T STOP IT
ON YOUR OWN!

---

(6) ADDICTION

No matter how many times or how hard one tries to quit their substance abuse on their own but continually returns to "out of control" use, they have an addiction! There are several key tenets to addiction which I often discuss with my clients, students and readers. Though they are not in any order of importance, as they are all important, these tenets describe the virtues of addiction in its raw and purest form:

1) **The addict has tried to quit on their own repeatedly and can't without some outside intervention/help. Thinking you can do it alone is magical thinking!**

2) **Addictions do not discriminate!**

3) It is a progressive and insidious disease which happens over time. It does not just develop into an addiction overnight!

4) The user/addict develops a tolerance for the substance, whether it be psychological, physiological, or both. They need more of the same substance or stronger doses to get the same favorable sensation.

5) Individuals experience withdrawal symptoms as soon as they try to stop using. These might be either physiological or psychological. When it is in the bloodstream, brain chemistry or hormonal system, then you know it is physical because the body goes into physical withdrawal.

6) Individuals will traverse through psychological stages before, during and after treatment and recovery. Moods and behaviors run the entire gambit of emotions from highs (euphoria) to lows (depression, even suicidal thoughts). In many cases the addict resembles someone with bi-polar mood disorders and in some cases they have bi-polar depression.

7) Relapse is often times a part of the recovery process. Slips and falls are a part of the healing process, as they teach lessons and help the addict identify triggers.

8) Some individuals use substances because it provides them a means of instant gratification or a quick fix.

9) **Some individuals become psychologically conditioned to use due to environment, social factors or triggers which stimulate the use/abuse of the substance. Sometimes it is not the drug/substance itself that provides the greatest stimulation rather the environment.**

10) **Some individuals engage in substance use to alleviate emotional or physical pain and enjoy the rapid numbing relief the drug/substance provides. In the world of addiction this is referred to as self-medication.**

11) **The availability or easy access of the substance creates a stimulus to use the drug. Sometimes when something is this there, it perpetuates the desire/need to use which wouldn't otherwise occur.**

12) **Being healed or cured is part of the recovery process. Only one in recovery can determine and acknowledge when they are truly healed or cured, or if they are in a state of ongoing "recovery".**

13) **Some individuals with addictions possess the addiction because they have a mental health disorder which perpetuates the addiction. On the other hand, through repeated use leading to addiction, eventually the addiction/substance use has perpetuated a mental health problem/illness.**

ADDICTIVE PERSONALITIES

There are certain people who are more prone to becoming addicts than other people. Perhaps you might refer to them as having "addictive personalities". Their childhood experiences as well as their family backgrounds may have created triggers or learning patterns which lead them to engage in compulsive and/or addictive behaviors. This of course rules out biological components, i.e. biological predispositions which make them at risk as well.

For whatever reason, certain people who possess addictive personality types rarely if ever find satisfaction or fulfillment in endeavors they engage in. Even if they never went on to develop an addiction, they would always be looking for something to provide them with pleasurable sensations. They will do whatever it takes to avoid pain – being or feeling responsible for changing their negative patterns and lifestyles. Having to look within themselves is too painful!

Over the years I found one thing common in many addicts as well as individuals suffering from mental health disorders...they believe if they ignore the problem or distract themselves from the problem, i.e. using alcohol or drugs, the problem will go away on its own. Ironically, the use of alcohol or drugs which could eventually lead to addiction creates a whole new set of problems, usually ones not as intense as the original. When addicts go into treatment and possess concurrent disorders (an addiction plus a mental health disorder) it is sometimes hard to determine which came first, the mental health illness or the addiction. Avoidance of problem solving in essence creates the chicken and egg dilemma – which came first?

The longer individuals engage in avoidance, or ignoring the problem, the less likely they are to possess any problem solving skills they might have had. Even if the skills were minimal, it gave them some sense of control in solving problems. It gave them confidence! At this point, any confidence and self-esteem they had bottoms out and this lacking of self-ability leads to an entirely new level of avoidance.

In the end, individuals with addictive personalities will avoid relationships like the plague. Since they have a hard time forming them and maintaining them, they are more likely to isolate themselves and engage in substance use/abuse which provides pleasurable sensations. Getting high or drunk masks and/or distracts their feelings of perceived rejection. Ironically, they are usually the ones doing the rejecting because they don't want to allow anyone to get too close to them because the others will see through them and into their emptiness – using substances to try to fulfill them.

Since addicts will never find fulfillment from the substances they are using to provide instant gratification, and since they can't maintain a relationship, they never know any true state of happiness or contentment. In essence, it is a vicious cycle they create for themselves in trying to latch onto someone or something to give them some sense of meaning in their lives.

TOLERANCE IN ADDICTION

Many addicts will develop a tolerance to the substance they choose to base their addiction around. Larger doses will be needed to provide the same effect. This can come in one of two ways; the individual may increase the dosage of their target substance, or the individual might increase the frequency through which they use the substance. Generally, when drug tolerances are discussed it is always in the context of physiological tolerance – the body develops a tolerance to the substance. Since many addictions are also non-drug based, i.e. pornography, sex, gambling, etc., the tolerance one develops need not only be physiological as it can be psychological as well. For example, an individual with a pornography addiction may feel like they are going crazy (agitated, frustrated and even desperate) if they don't get their daily fix of porn. Even though the pornography is not a drug, it affects the body/mind as if it were a drug. This is a psychological addiction.

The tolerance can be either physiologically-based, psychologically-based or a combination of both. One of the more interesting addictions I have worked with is cigarette/nicotine addictions. Over the years I have helped many clients quit smoking through hypnosis, cognitive behavioral therapy, or a combination of both. The reason I find cigarette addiction to be a complex addiction is it usually can be any of the mentioned types of tolerances. Let me explain using all 3 types of tolerance options:

1) Physiological addiction - The individual smokes because they require the desired effect the nicotine (stimulant) has on their brain. They are used to having nicotine in their blood/brain and this is needed to alter their mood and help them function. Whenever they do not get their daily scheduled smokes, they have "nic fits" whereby they get the shakes, feel jittery, feel light-headed, extremely moody and agitated and feel as if they cannot function. Once they have the smoke, they feel better...instantly! The body needs the nicotine.

2) Psychological addiction - The individual usually smokes after they have their first coffee, on the drive into work, in social settings, or whenever they have a chance. When asked about their smoking schedule, most of these smokers will assert they can go for long periods of time without smoking and not feel like they are coming undone. They more or less "believe they need" the cigarette to provide some sort of pleasure or instant gratification. You see, it is based on "believing" you need to smoke!

3) Physiological and psychological addiction - The individual needs to smoke to crave the withdrawal symptoms that the body is experiencing as well as believing they need to smoke to satisfy cravings beforehand or provide instant gratification. Sometimes the body just needs the nicotine, while other times it is more mind over matter – feeling the need to just have a smoke.

Without getting into all of the facets of smoking cessation as there are great books on the subjects, I just want to point out two things I have noticed over the last 17 years of doing this.

First, if a person can quit smoking cold turkey and have minimal to zero physiological effects, then they probably had a psychological addiction to smoking. I have had friends and colleagues quit on the first attempt and never do it again. I have seen women find out they were pregnant and quit without batting an eyelash and having no withdrawal symptoms. This would tell me they had a psychological addiction versus a physiological addiction. With that said, they might have had aspects of a physiological addiction of smoking, but they were able to exert incredible "mind over matter" and quit. In the study of neuropsychoimmunology or psychosomatics, their minds ruled and minimized or abolished any and all physical cravings/withdrawal symptoms.

Second, if and when I used hypnosis to help clients quit smoking and if it worked first time out, or second time, then once again it was probably more of a psychological addiction. I will add that the post-hypnotic suggestions I provided enhance psychosomatic powers in the mind. With that said, the mind might have mastered the ability to control their body (robot) and tell it what to do. I have found that hypnosis only works on habits and psychological type addictions if they are not too severe. In hard addictions like alcohol, heroin, etc., it rarely works because the physiological tolerance is too great and hypnosis does not get down to the underlying, deep-rooted psychological issues which are causing the self-destructive behaviors. Having said that, I do believe that hypnosis over a prolonged period of time combined with cognitive behavioral therapy (CBT) can be extremely successful in treating hard addictions only if three things occur; 1) the individual goes through a detox programme at the onset of treatment, 2) hypnotherapy and CBT are used ongoing throughout the therapeutic process and 3) the individual is open to attending support groups. I believe in differential diagnosis – every individual personality is unique as are their experiences. What may work for one may not work for another. You can never disqualify a treatment because it worked or didn't work for someone. I truly believe if an individual with an addiction was to apply all three components of the aforementioned treatment, they would be highly successful in their recovery!

WITHDRAWAL IN ADDICTION

In addiction, withdrawal is best described as the intense group of symptoms one experiences when they suddenly or abruptly stop using their substance of choice. Since the individual has been using/abusing the substance for such a long period of time, their body and/or mind becomes dependent upon the effects that the substance provides, or the satisfaction they get from engaging in using the substance. When the individual does not get their "fix" they will start to feel worse and begin to engage in desperate acts to satiate themselves and make the withdrawal symptoms go away. If they continue to spiral into the withdrawal symptoms, they will eventually dissipate and hit a wall or plateau and not get any worse. If the individual can make it to this plateau and stay clean, then they are basically in a "detox" stage leading to sobriety. This is what is needed for therapy and recovery to be effective.

As with tolerance, the withdrawal symptoms can be any of the three in nature; 1) physiological, 2) psychological or 3) physiological and psychological. Individuals with intense addictions (alcohol, heroin, cocaine, etc.) need to detox and reach plateau in their withdrawal symptoms to turn the corner.

I've given you a lot of information in this chapter on habit versus addiction. Having said that, I have only scratched the surface. There are exceptional books and information out there which describe/define addiction in greater depth. I highly recommend visiting the following websites on the Internet to become more familiar with addictions. I have had the good fortunes of working with the following organizations in the past or present and highly recommend their research:

Centre for Addiction and Mental Health (CAMH) – *http://www.camh.net/*
Mayo Clinic – *http://www.mayoclinic.com/*
Betty Ford Clinic – *http://www.bettyfordcenter.org/*
Homewood Health Centre – *http://www.homewood.org/healthcentre/main.php*
Renascent Toronto – *http://www.renascent.ca/*

CHAPTER TWO:

MAKING SENSE OF CONCURRENT DISORDERS

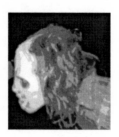

"An intelligent person is never afraid or ashamed to find errors in his understanding of things."

Bryant H. McGill

In the last chapter, I brought up the notion of concurrent disorders as they related to addiction. For the purpose of this chapter, I would like to go a little more in depth in describing what a concurrent disorder is for those who are hearing about this concept for the first time or have a minimal understanding for what it is.

A concurrent disorder is when the illness combines both a mental health problem and a substance use problem. In the USA and other parts of the world it is often times referred to as a dual disorder, dual diagnosis or co-morbidity. For the purpose of this chapter and any future references to this concept will be labeled as "concurrent disorder". I am discussing concurrent disorders briefly in this book as I want to show you where irrational thinking patterns as well as negative cognitive scripts tend to create, perpetuate or reinforce BITTER RESISTANCE.

So, what came first...the chicken or the egg? This question has haunted humans from the dawning of civilization until now, well at least sort of. The answer is usually who cares once you crack the egg in the frying pan or roast the chicken in the oven. Either way, the end results in something being cooked, boiled, roasted, barbequed, scrambled or fried. It doesn't matter what came first, rather it reached a final point – cooked! The same can be said about concurrent disorders. It doesn't matter what came first, the mental illness or the addiction, or whether they arrived at the same time. The end result is the individual usually feels cooked, boiled, roasted, barbequed, scrambled or fried! So it's not really a matter of worrying about what came first, rather more about why something came to be and more importantly doing the only thing you can control...working in the here and now. The only thing anyone truly ever has any control over is what they are thinking in the moment which leads to how they are feeling in that moment.

I am a firm believer in simultaneous treatment for concurrent disorders – treating the mental health problem and the addiction at the same time. Each is a trigger and/or facilitator for the other at this point in the addiction process. There is no sense in splitting hairs trying to figure out what came first at this point. The key is immediate treatment in order to bring the individual to a point of healthy and rational functioning. Once you have reached this point, then it is okay to poke your head back into the past, just for a bit not to get fixated on what happened in terms of victimization, rather to understand the causal-effect relationship which preceded the addiction and/or mental health problem for the purpose of identifying triggers and of course BITTERNESS!

From leading support groups as well as doing individual counseling, two things I believe are required for optimal success when treating concurrent disorders:

1) Whenever the individual is in full blown substance, alcohol or drug use and it has created the utmost physiological addiction where they can't function without their drug as it makes them physically or mentally ill without it, then they should first undergo detoxification. If the individual is suffering from DT's, hallucinations and delusional thinking from the substance/alcohol, they need to be clear for any kind of therapeutic process to be effective.

2) Whenever the individual has severe mental health problems that create intense delusional thinking, or disjointed rationalizations, then they need to receive the proper medication under the supervision of a psychiatrist who understands the mental health problem and how the pharmaceutical medication will provide optimal, positive effects. There are those who believe any and all drugs are bad, however, if the individual suffers from full blown bi-polar depression, dysthymia or schizophrenia then they need medication to stabilize them and help them to function normally. I have worked with individuals with the aforementioned mental health illnesses without receiving medication and I would have been better off talking to a wall. On the other hand, once they were treated with the right medication, it was like night and day – the ability to treat them

with CBT was so smooth and effective. Positive results were seen almost immediately in terms of grasping the therapy and applying it to their immediate thought process.

The key to treating concurrent disorders, first and foremost, is to always make sure the individual is in a state of readiness, physically and mentally. If they are not it is like whistling in the wind. You do not want to set anyone up for failure as these folks probably have had enough failures already to last them a lifetime. When it comes to failing at treatment, it might be enough to push them away from any future treatment for a long time or ever!

I do want to clarify that I am not saying that one's past is not relevant to where they are because it definitely is. Sure you want to unlock the underlying negative images that are still affixed to whatever is producing the mental health illness and/or addiction, but not dwell on it for an eternity. Some therapists would have clients lie on their couches and rehash their pasts starting with childhood and working from there forward chronologically to where they are now. Do you have any idea how much time that takes, pun intended? It is just too frustrating for some and may take years to get true results. Ideally, a good therapist would employ a CBT based approach which is definitely client-centered based as well. I should mention that I am very CBT biased as that was my background training having studied with the father of RET (Rational Emotive Therapy) Albert Ellis, as well as having gotten to know William Glasser (creator of Reality Therapy) over the years. All I know is it works – clients function better faster and have a greater propensity toward their own positive self-efficacy!

The goal for treatment of concurrent disorders is to get the client functioning as effectively as possible in the shortest time. As clients become more productive and successful taking baby steps (to borrow a line from the movie *What About Bob* which I loved!) they also become more confident in their decision-making skills and life style choices. You see, to become an addict or not to become an addict is all based on choices...to use or not to use. CBT employs the ability to recognize irrational or destructive thought patterns and helps client see greater options. When you do something repeatedly for a period of time, you start to believe there aren't any other options. Getting clients "clear" in their thinking teaches them to think abstractly and see greater options. Over time, through repeated use and abuse of substances, many addicts develop the ability to create blinders to the consequences of their use. In terms of cause-effect relationships, it might look something like this:

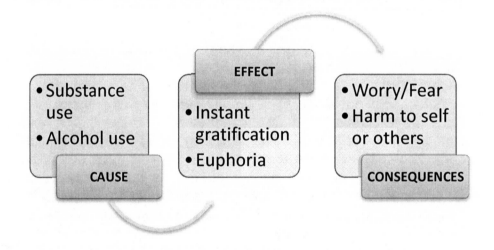

ONSET OF SUBSTANCE USE/ABUSE

   * The individual views consequences abstractly. Their consequences/moral reasoning is based in fear and worry. They worry about getting caught if they are doing something illegally. They worry about compromising their own health and believe they can engage the activity using moderation management. They worry about getting caught by family members and getting in trouble and/or hurting them. They worry about their jobs.

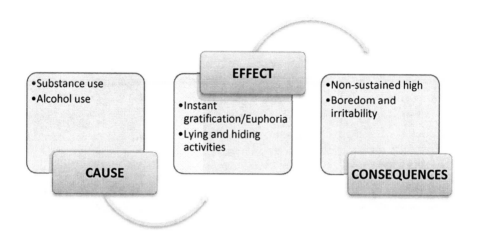

BEGINNING OF AN ADDICTION

*In this state, individuals view the consequences less abstractly and more based on greed – instant gratification and maintaining a state of highness/euphoria. The consequences are perceived as more self-serving in their lying and hiding of their activities surrounding their addiction. It's not about hurting others or themselves as much as not getting caught. If they get caught, then they might be forced to stop using. This produces fear!

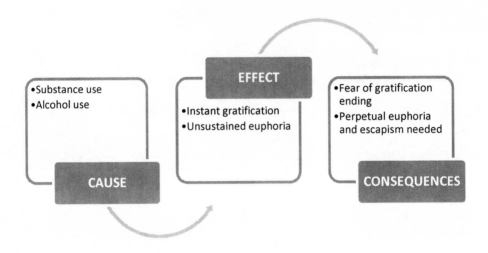

FULL BLOWN ADDICTION

* In the case of the full-blown addict, consequences are marginal at best. All consequences are based of survival, not of "self" but keeping/maintaining the addiction. By this point, a sense of guilt, shame and remorse are usually minimal at best towards self and others with doing whatever it takes to use being the major priority. The only real consequence they see is "having to quit" which they are not ready for.

When you plug a mental health disorder into the equation which facilitates, perpetuates or becomes a by-product of the addiction, irrational and faulty thinking patterns are more readily produced. At this point, when an individual becomes a full-blown addict, their abilities to think rationally, see consequences of their actions abstractly and identify both short-term and long-term negative outcomes are diminished. The notion of self becomes one rooted in survival, the need to maintain their addiction as the addiction itself becomes blending as being one with them, or even what they believe they have become...the addict. If you remove the substance from them, then they believe you are removing "the self" from them and in essence, you are taking away their identity!

One of the greatest conundrums with concurrent disorders is that it presents the individual with a double-edged sword...they are both ends! You see, individuals who are just "addicts" will eventually come to view themselves in light of their addiction as I discussed above. The addiction swallows their identity and self. Similarly, many individuals with mental health illnesses begin to identify with their illness and the concept of self becomes one with the illness. Many professionals like myself shy away from the labeling effect. No one wants to be named, "Schizo", "Manic", "Anorexic", "Crackhead", "Drunk", and even "Alcoholic". You see, the name/label says a lot about a person. People often live according to the names and labels they are given. Don't believe me? There is countless research on self-esteem issues related to verbal/mental abuse in kids. Guess what? Most of this is name-calling. Adults are not different... words/labels hurt! I know individuals who are alcoholics will announce at A.A. meetings, "Hi, I'm Joe and I am an alcoholic." I get that they use it to remind themselves of what they have and what they came from, but that is not that person. They are not the "alcoholic"; rather, they have an addiction to alcohol. In my own practice in the past treating clients I would encourage them rather to refer to themselves as either, "Hi, I am Joe and I am recovering from my alcoholism!" or, "Hi, I am Joe and I am in recovery!" You see, words like "recovery" are empowering, positive, action words. It reminds the individual they are in a state of action and in control. Furthermore, they are not identified with the illness or being the illness. Also, the illness (full blown addiction) is in the past. If one is in recovery, they are not "addiction" or an "addict" rather a person of "recovery"!

Individuals with concurrent disorders get the double-whammy! Unfortunately they get two portions of diverse labels. If their lives weren't already confusing enough these labels add to greater complications.

There is no doubt that most individuals with addictions either have a mental health problem or several components of one. Conversely, most with mental health problems do not have an addiction. However with that said, many do possess obsessive thinking patterns as well as some compulsions which could lead them to addiction. When their addictive personalities are not held in check and the mental illness overwhelms them, then the addiction has the ability to flourish. Some individuals might become addicted to their prescription drugs – either psychologically or physically dependent on them. With that said, there are many individuals with mental health disorders who by all accounts have addictions (prescribed drugs) but slip under the radar since they are not using alcohol, recreational drugs or other forms of substances.

I just wanted to scratch the surface in this chapter discussing concurrent disorders and introduce it to those not familiar with the concept. Having said that, I believe there is so much wonderful new information available on concurrent disorders. To learn about concurrent disorders in greater depth, I highly recommend and/or all of the following agencies/websites:

CAMH – http://www.camh.net/
STEMSS –
http://kap.samhsa.gov/products/manuals/taps/17k.htm

Mayo Clinic – http://www.mayoclinic.com/health/drug-addiction/DS00183

CHAPTER THREE:

BITTER RESISTANCE

"Resentment is like taking poison and waiting for the other person to die."

Malachy McCourt

How many people function each and every day with self-destructive mentalities? Furthermore, how many people live to cut off their own noses just to spite their faces? If this were a statistical quiz then perhaps I would need to come up with a number. With that said, I am just going to guess, too many! Are you one of those people?

Some say nothing makes a person feel more alive than to be angry-- at other people, at the world...at themselves. This anger gives them a sense of control, well at least a distorted, dysfunctional and disjointed sense of control. Ironically, the only things you can control in this scenario are the thoughts you think which lead to the feelings you feel. Ironically, most people despise feeling angry, bitter or resentful and can't seem to stop themselves.

In my book, _What's Your Anger Type?_, I identify twelve different types of anger. Of these twelve types, one I coined _Petrified Anger,_ which is the hallmark of bitterness. Even though I cite all types of anger as having purposes, some are worse than others in their abilities to create damage to lives. Petrified anger is one of the worst in its ability to create self-destruction in individuals!

What is petrified anger? People with petrified anger lock everything inside of themselves and start to cause themselves unnecessary suffering. Something happened to them in the past, a perceived wrong doing. They felt that someone hurt them intentionally, or a situation made them a "victim". They believed they were "wronged" and treated unfairly. Some part of them wanted retribution or restitution. Instead of letting it go and forgiving others or the situation, they hold onto it. Holding onto something, even bad feelings gives the individual some sense of control over the situation. You see, they possess a sense of ownership. However negative, sick or twisted this "holding on" is, it is better than nothing. This is their perceived way of holding onto the past – reliving it and trying to make sense of it or undoing it.

When you keep reliving the same event over again, you basically become like an individual who suffers from posttraumatic stress disorder (PTSD). This disorder carries with it some very unpleasant feelings and physical disorders:

~ <u>bitterness</u> ** (*one of the key premises of this book*)
~ flashbacks
~ depression
~ anxiety
~ fear
~ nausea/vomiting
~ insomnia
~ constant worrying
~ irritability
~ increased alcohol/drug consumption
~ bodily aches and pains
~ increased blood pressure
~ increased heart rate

In essence, petrified anger is like a mocked form of PTSD. The individual really truly believes they were victimized, abused or exploited.

What many individuals don't understand is that by reliving their experiences repetitiously, the mind tricks the body into believing the experience is real. The body reacts accordingly and prepares itself for fight mode. Over a period of time, you actually tax your body by putting it into what Walter Cannon called the "Fight or Flight Syndrome", where you keep creating adrenaline rushes which tax the central nervous system. Given time, the body could actually suffer from what Hans Selye found in his *General Adaptation Syndrome* model. In a very condensed form, this model asserts that the more we are in this "high state of alert" posturing, the more we drain ourselves and weaken our immune systems possibly causing serious or permanent damage. This produces tremendous feelings of frustration, anxiety and a lifestyle of always feeling "stressed out"! If this doesn't produce or lead to clinical diagnoses of mental health disorders, such as Generalized Anxiety Disorders, panic attacks and depression, these feelings are most likely very real and this is when individuals drink or drug to cope with or mask these symptoms. When this goes on for prolonged time frames, the individual is more likely to develop a concurrent disorder.

In my book, *What's Your Anger Type?*, I also discuss another type of anger closely resembling the by-products that petrified anger produces. This is called *Resistant/ Passive Anger.* The bottom line with this anger type is that individuals never feel good about themselves. The world is always unfair to them. They were dealt a bad hand of cards. There is some sort of conspiracy going on where everyone is against them. They just don't understand why things are the way things are. They have developed a method of self-defeating thinking and they have trapped themselves in a lazy, irrational, stereotypical way of perceiving the world.

Like petrified anger, resistant/passive anger leads individuals to develop a more passé approach to situations and people. Even though they do not like what others are doing to them or what is happening to them, they refuse to say something or correct the situation externally. They are conflict avoidant. Instead, they internalize their negative thoughts and feelings over the situation and allow them to fester. Even though they are angry and/or disagree with others, they don't say anything. They do not speak up because they feel uneasy over confrontation or expressing their honest feelings. They worry they will hurt others if they speak up, or others will not like them. Basically, they would rather "be seen and not heard" in terms of their feelings. I have worked with many individuals possessing this type of anger and their theme is, "I'd rather be accepted for all of the wrong reasons, than be alone for all of the right reasons – being alone sucks!"

Holding everything in with this type of anger produces the similar effects that petrified anger does. It not only wears the person out, but it also creates feelings of disdain even hatred for themselves! The precipitating cause is persistent or escalating stress in one's life which leads to unceasing frustration. Eventually, you get to the point where you can't take it anymore and reach meltdown. Individuals I have worked with have reported they feel like they are coming undone – having a nervous breakdown!

The feelings associated with this type of anger are taxing on the body/nervous system. Many people often report feeling any/or most of these symptoms:

~ *chronic fatigue*
~ *nausea/vomiting*
~ *constant colds*
~ *small aches/pains*
~ *feeling tired and run down*
~ *loss of appetite*
~ *sleep disturbances/insomnia*
~ *mental flashbacks*
~ *frequent crying spells*
~ *suicidal thoughts*
~ *social isolation/withdrawing*
~ *drinking/drug use*
~ *pessimism*
~ *irrational fears*
~ *depression*

Depression appears to be the most common by-product of resistant anger. Individuals are so pre-occupied with not being angry that they become highly focused on the emotion unconsciously. Consequently, what happens is the anger is turned inward and manifests itself in the form of depression. Rather than expel the negative feelings which are building inside them, they hold onto them and try to extinguish them on the inside. Sure, the anger gets watered down; however, it becomes diluted into a more "acceptable" emotion... depression!

Think about this for a moment! What emotion is more likely to receive greater empathy and sympathy: anger or depression? If you're angry, people avoid you because they perceive you as dangerous. On the other hand, if you are depressed, you are perceived to be less of a threat. In fact, people will actually start to feel sorry for you and actually enable your depression. So you actually get to be "accepted" more readily for being depressed. Being depressed serves a purpose – being accepted as a victim!

Some individuals with resistant anger could be classified as possessing an almost "sadomasochistic" lifestyle. The only time they feel alive is when they are "in pain" or complaining about something. Working with clients in support groups and one on one, these are some of the behavioral attributes individuals with this anger type display:

~ Allowing others to make decisions for them.
~ Feeling used and unappreciated.
~ Frustrating to others because they show no initiative or assertion.
~ Saying yes when they want to say no.
~ Being in situations they don't want to be in.
~ Blaming others for their unhappiness.
~ Constantly seeking other's approval.
~ Feeling like every situation is the same.

The end result of accepting and using this "anger" method is ultimate frustration and stress leading to depression. When this overwhelms the individual they are most likely to turn to alcohol or drugs to shut the mind off and eliminate the negative feelings that eat away at them. Behaving passively over years has the ability to produce and promote feelings of learned helplessness. This is often times the catalyst for depression.

Through mental repetitions and cognitive scripting we become who we are based on what we think about most. If you think that you are a good person then you will believe you are a good person. If you think you deserve the best that life has to offer, then you will work towards getting the best and being grateful that it is a part of your life. Conversely, if you think thoughts about being and feeling worthless, and that you don't deserve better – life has dealt you a terrible hand, then this will become your reality and you will act and become accordingly. When you add all of this stuff together (What I have discussed in this chapter so far) the seeds of *BITTERNESS* have been sown and through repetition, the fertilizer called *RESISTANCE TO CHANGE* makes sure it flourishes and stays alive. The end result is **<u>BITTER RESISTANCE</u>**!

Perhaps one of the greatest idiosyncrasies in addictions is "reasoning". The downfall for most individuals possessing addictions is they become addicted to reasoning. Furthermore, their reasoning is usually extremely faulty based on the bitterness that underlies it. Reasoning becomes clouded by emotion which complicates things for them. Throw in one's ego and things get utterly complicated!

All humans crave reason. They need to know the "why's" and "how's" for how things turn out the way they do. Humans do this based on what they are taught early in life – cause/effect relationships. They know that everything happens for a reason, that there is an underlying cause which created the outcome. Simply put: Minds require a sense of order!

The sense of order is arrived at by analyzing the cause/effect relationship. Minds need to make sense of it and this sense is derived from previous experiences as well as the current analytical skills the individual possesses. The mind doesn't discern whether or not the reasoning skills are accurate or faulty. It processes them all the same due to repetition. It is one's ego that has the ability to change the thought process and discern whether or not it is working effectively. As long as the ego thinks or believes one's thought process is working effectively, it will continue to accept things as they are and always were.

Feeling comfortable is a great feeling for almost everyone. If they feel great about themselves and they are functional in their everyday lives, then they keep things as they are. Their egos govern their choices (thoughts and feelings) and keeps things status quo. Interestingly, the same holds true for individuals with dysfunctional lives. The dysfunction in their lives can actually be comforting. They would rather dance with the devil they know (negative thoughts, addiction and mental health illness) than risk change and improving which is frightening and can be overwhelming in they fail at change. Regardless, even if something provides comfort and it is wrong, it doesn't make it right. It is just a momentary fix to the long-term problem (irrational thought processes).

Now to embrace this dysfunctional zone of comfort provides a crutch of sorts. This "crutch" is a victim's mentality – "Why me?", "Woe is me!" mindset. You see, whenever things turn out bad, they can always play the victim's role of "Why me?" Ironically, this "Why me?" mindset was seeded a long time ago when they felt or were victimized and derived some good from it. Perhaps their anger became petrified toward the event as well as others and from this they became more passive – the victim!

Some people believe that being the victim is the place to be. It lets them off easy, at least in their own minds. They might get sympathy from others, or others might enable their dysfunctional behavior. They perceive this as permission or encouragement to continue. Their egos latch onto this and create cognitive scripts or repetition compulsions around this dysfunction. At the end of the day they truly believe they are entitled, encouraged and expected to act this way. And in some cases they are if they are in a codependent relationship or enmeshed family where others hold power over them as they play the victim.

Some people constantly live in the past, flogging a dead horse – what happened to them. They feel the need to analyze everything until their heads spin in utter confusion. What happens is all rational reasoning and logic is displaced by their emotions. Since the emotion usually dominates them, these folks begin to start identifying with the emotion rather than the thoughts they tried to dissect. When you don't let go of something and hang onto it for a long time, neuropathways in the brain get melted in and when you have the same thoughts, they immediately trigger the same feelings by default. Before you have a chance to recognize what is happening when you think that negative thought from the past, the feeling kicks in, dominates and the individual is left to deal with the feelings which usually swallow them up. When emotions get tangled in with a victim's mentality, they usually win. Trying to relive the past and figure things out is a recipe for disaster!

In the famous movie *A Few Good Men*, Jack Nicholson's character shouts at Tom Cruise's character in the courtroom, "You can't handle the truth!" Oh, how true this is for many! Sometimes you should be mindful not to mention careful of what you want to know as it may open a larger can of worms. Someone with a mindset of BITTER RESISTANCE wants to know...all of the time! You see, reasoning, whether it be rational or irrational, provides a perceived sense of control for them. For some, analyzing things to the bone is the only way they can achieve a sense of control over their lives. Even though they will never have control in this sense (Going back and changing the past), the racing thoughts which produce intense feelings bring them back to that place in time and they relive it. This makes them feel as if they are alive and their irrational and unconscious cognitive scripts trick them into believing that if they do this enough times, just maybe the outcome will turn out different. Not! And this is where and when ego comes in!

Bitter resistance is all based on ego. In this case, their egos are fragmented. They have an inability to integrate all parts of themselves together. It is almost as if an individual creates a dual self, or two separate aspects of themselves – their true self and their ego.

First I want to clarify what I mean when I am referring to ego in this book. I want ego to mean the generic term of "I" or "self-concept" which one carries for oneself. This "ego" differs from the concept Sigmund Freud coined in the three aspects or parts of personality he referred to as ID, EGO and SUPER EGO. In Freud's model, all three aspects (ID, EGO and SUPEREGO) overlap and interact to form the personality. See diagram below:

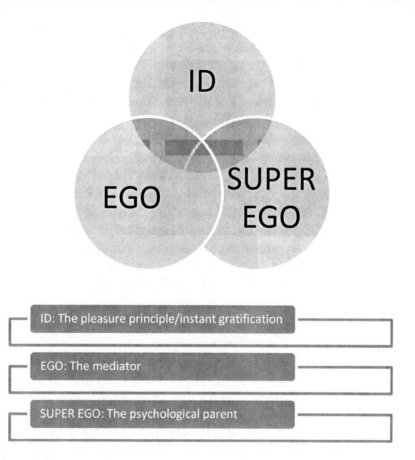

ID: The pleasure principle/instant gratification

EGO: The mediator

SUPER EGO: The psychological parent

In Freud's conceptualization of personality; ID, EGO and SUPER EGO, Freud discussed the ego as being the mediator. The mediator's job is to remain in the present (here and now) mindset and guide the individual into making rational choices. According to Freud's theory, the ego as mediator diminishes in its capacity to be effective whenever the id or super ego is more dominant.

If you use Freud's framework for personality, the id is the key component which precipitates the need for instant gratification. In general, people who suffer with addictions often times possess very overwhelming ids. The id operates on the pleasure principle and demands things in the "now" without any regard for future consequences. If you remember, "desire" catapults one to try and eventually continue to use their substance of choice. The reason desire is so strong in addiction based on Freud's theory, is that they have an overwhelming id which rules and/or controls the ego (mediator).

Conversely, the super ego serves as the psychological parent individuals carry around with them. This tells them what is "right" versus "wrong" and weighs in the consequences to serve as deterrents for wrongful behavior. When the ego is balanced and able to mediate, the super ego points out "wrongs" and allows the individual to engage in rational decision making. When the super ego rules the roost, then it creates within the individual a platform of guilt from which they operate. Everything they do tends to be over-analyzed and magnified. The by-product of this is obsessing and repetition compulsion. This leads to an obsessive-compulsive mindset thus creating intense feelings of anxiety, panic, frustration/anger and eventually depression.

Freud's theory of personality is exceptional when you apply it to addiction which would assert the individual has a weakened ego that is over-run by either the id or super ego or both. The feelings and reasons one uses substances based on the id is different from the reasons they do if they are super ego based. When you add both to the equation, you get full-blown concurrent disordered individuals. See diagram below:

FREUDIAN PERSONALITY MODEL EXPLAINING ADDICTION/ SUBSTANCE USE:

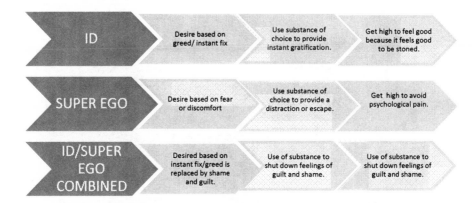

In all three scenarios the ego (mediator) is non-existent or diminished in its capabilities to do its job. The individual becomes a substances user because they are either "ID" driven, "SUPER EGO" driven or a combination of both. When it is "ID" driven, they live for the here/now and need a quick fix just to feel good. They do not worry about the consequences afterward. When the individual is "SUPER EGO" driven, they live in a state of guilt, shame or worry. They use or become addicted to the substance of choice as a way of coping or functioning as they can't shut off the obsessive thoughts they have. In the worst case scenario where they are "ID/SUPER EGO" driven, they are caught in between a rock and a hard place. Their id wants them to use because "it will feel good" but their super ego chastises them for thinking that and they drown in feelings of guilt and shame for feeling that way. In order to shut off the id which keeps pestering them to use and the super ego which keeps tormenting them psychologically with punitive thoughts, they use the substance of their choice to shut things down. In this cycle, concurrent disorders are more likely to become prevalent! In all three situations a cycle of use and addiction is perpetuated!

If you apply Freud's personality to reflect a strong ego that has the ability to control and mediate, the outcome would be as follows in the diagram below:

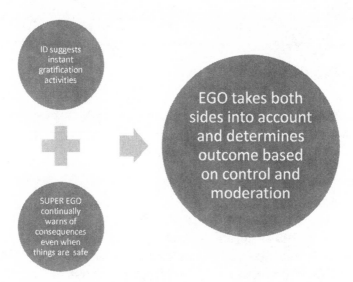

In this scenario, a healthy and strong ego helps the individual remain in a state of balance and harmony. They are less likely to become addicted to substances and/or develop a mental health illness.

For the purpose of this book and to explain BITTER RESISTANCE, I will now turn over the discussion on EGO to mean "self" and ability to make choices. I will not use ID or SUPER EGO to compliment EGO. Instead, when I refer to one's ego it will mean their self-concept which leads them into the choices they make.

In the diagram below I have demonstrated how the EGO/SELF-CONCEPT is comprised of the four components which make up the biological/psychological/social and spiritual model.

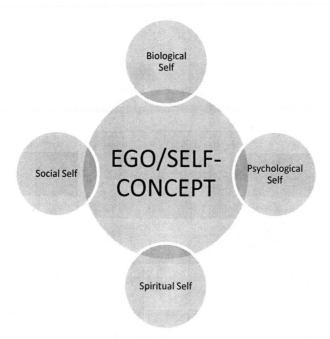

You see, EGO/SELF is always at the centre of its universe. It determines how one interacts with not only one's surroundings, but one's inner dialogue as well.

Take a moment and sit back in a quiet area. Now with eyes closed, focus on your moment to moment awareness. Pay attention to your inner dialogue. What are your thoughts saying? If you could "guess-timate" the number of negative thoughts you had while doing this exercise (say for 5 minutes) what percentage of your thoughts would be of the negative variety? These negative thoughts would include anything that produces feelings of; anger, fear, anxiety, resentment, worry or depression. One thing to take into account – what we think about most we will draw more to us in terms of thoughts. If we think negative thoughts we are certain to bring fresh batches of negative thoughts and then some into the centre of our thought processes.

> **BITTER RESISTANCE** – The same negative thoughts that continue to flourish perpetuate and increase negative thinking scripts, which are based on an unfortunate incident or negatively perceived event from the past. This cognitive script becomes engrained in the mind and held onto as truth, leading individuals to become addicted (obsessed) with the memory which leads them to addictive behaviours to try and quiet the mind.

An individual's ego can trick an individual into believing they need to place their focus on something even though they really don't need to, or should not because it is more detrimental than good. Have you ever heard of the expression, "Out of sight, out of mind..."? If an individual could apply this principle to their thought process which centres on bitter resistance thoughts, they have already achieved half of their battle. They have been able to devoid their focus from what they don't want and will be able to point their minds in the direction of what they do want – freedom and sweet acceptance. It sounds so easy, but why don't people just do it? EGO–

The ego tricks people into thinking that they are always in control. For all intents and purposes, we truly are in control all of the time; that is, in control of what we choose to think and feel. And here is where the hypocrisy arises. Even though the ego wants to be in control and does its best to dominate, it creates the thoughts that it doesn't want to think about but in the same instance it tricks the individual into thinking they are helpless – a victim!

Resentment
is like taking poison and hoping the other person dies.
~ St. Augustine

Here is a simple quick experiment. Lemon, lemon... Okay don't think about lemons! How easy is it to not think about lemons after you've basically become a part of the "ade"? I use the example of "lemons" as well to denote the famous saying...When life hands you lemons make lemonade! Unfortunately, the motto of individuals who suffer from bitter resistance is more of the mindset that, when life hands you lemons, squeeze them in the eyes of your enemies! You see, individuals operating from framework of bitter resistance focus on negative aspects of the past, dwell on it and allow it to crystallize into embittered cognitive scripts.

I am a huge advocate for Cognitive Behavioural Therapy (CBT). I was extremely fortunate to have had the opportunity to receive personal training from the father of RET (Rational Emotive Therapy) and for all intents and purposes the greatest proponent of CBT, Albert Ellis. In his countless books on CBT/RET Ellis always brought to the forefront irrational thinking based on twisted perceptions of current events that happen in someone's life. Furthermore, he asserted this creates cognitive scripts and beliefs of current and future events – people react based on their interpretations and perceptions of the past. They carry this with them and use them as short-cut to their perceptions instead of actually looking at each new situation as being unique. No matter how unfavourable or favourable an event is, it is always weighted against past conclusions.

I am not going to dive into RET or Ellis, but will show you briefly how RET works:

IRRATIONAL THINKING CYCLE

In this progression, **A** represents the current event one is experiencing in the here and now. This is what is happening to the individual. When you move into the next segment, **B**, the individual forms a belief about **A**. This belief about **A** is carried forward from the past – using previous perceptions to form a present judgement even if it is irrational. When you move into **C**, the individual begins to emote feelings about **A**. Interestingly, these feelings usually have nothing to do with what is going on in **A**; rather, they are strongly biased and created by **B**. Most people only recognise the feelings which arise in the **C** part. Furthermore, those who have bitter resistance only acknowledge the feelings arising in **C** as being a by-product of **A**. With that said **D** becomes the section where individuals need to challenge the real reason they are feeling the way they are – uncovering and disputing the negative and embittered beliefs in **B**. As Ellis used to say, the feelings are not important in getting to the root of the issue and correcting it, rather you have to dispute the irrational beliefs that keep re-creating the negative feelings!

At the root of the matter for **B** are the irrational beliefs about oneself which creates and perpetuates the negative, unchallenged belief system. And these irrational beliefs can best be summed up by 4 words: **Disgusting, Worthless, Wrong and Bad!** These are the beliefs individuals possessing bitter resistance have come to accept of themselves and the core of their being. When things go wrong, or they perceive things going wrong, they personalize the situation and magnify these negative beliefs about themselves. This kicks the ball rolling and feelings collect like a snowball running downhill. Once it collects in size and momentum examining or challenging the feelings becomes a difficult task as it is ignored all together. The feelings become so overwhelming and discomforting that the only way to shut them down is to numb, distract or mask them by using alcohol or drugs. Bitter resistance only continues to multiply and mature in its negative capacity for allowing one's life to feel like it is out of control.

Now what? How does one get out of this? They need to embrace a state of **<u>SWEET ACCEPTANCE</u>**!

CHAPTER FOUR:

SWEET ACCEPTANCE

"The best road to progress is freedom's road."

John F. Kennedy

Can anyone ever be truly free from their past? The answer is YES! No one can literally live in their past because that is time gone that you can never get back. The only things you can live in the past are the experiences that your mind chooses to focus on. Even though they were real events that happened in the past, they are no longer real today because they don't exist. It is that simple!

In the last chapter I discussed bitter resistance which is a state of mind people choose. This is the current reality individuals select so they can recapitulate the negative and destructive feelings they harbour in their minds. The key concepts here are "choose" and "select". This means you have a choice to think, feel, act and become what it is you truly want to have. Your current reality (circumstances) are not who you truly are!

One of the exercises I have clients and students complete is an exercise in "intention shifting". The goal here is to get clients to take the negative energies they are focusing on and feeding and adjust them so they become positive energies.

INTENTIONAL SHIFTING: Taking your focus off of what you don't want and putting it on what you do want.

In intentional shifting, most people who suffer from bitter resistance are constantly focusing on those things that annoy, frustrate or disturb them, which adds greater fuel to the fire and brings more of those feelings and experiences to them. By intentionally shifting their energies, they are able to "intend" for a new set of pleasant, positive feelings which will manifest what they really want in their lives.

The exercise is extremely simple, as people are doing it all of the time. The problem is most do it by proxy and don't even realize they are drawing more experiences into their lives whether they are good or bad. So how does it work?

Use the table below to make a list of things that you don't want and then add the corresponding feelings:

THINGS I DON'T WANT!	THESE THINGS I DON'T WANT MAKE ME FEEL...

Now the goal in this exercise is to make lists of things that you don't want that are currently in your life, or you perceive as currently existing. Once you have made this list, read over it. What is most important is focusing on the right hand column (the feelings) and really feel how "what you don't want" is currently affecting your thinking and feeling. The feelings are probably intense. The more intense the feelings the more "bad feelings" of the same level or worse you are going to attract. This creates and perpetuates more bitter resistance!

Now I want you to take a minute to just relax, clear your head and emotions before moving onto the next little exercise. In this exercise, you are going to do the reverse and embrace a set of different feelings, some might even feel foreign or even "not right for you" because you do not feel worthy or deserving of them. When you are listing the feelings, really get into the feeling of having it – what would it feel like?

Okay, in the current moment, make a list under the following headings:

THINGS I WANT!	THESE THINGS I WANT MAKE ME FEEL...

In completing this list the second time, how did it make you "feel"? Did you feel really good about believing that what you wanted could be a reality for you? How long did it take for negative feelings to come washing in on you, flooding you with thoughts like; "It will never happen!", "I never get good breaks!", "I don't want to feel good because I will only be disappointed in the end!", or "I don't deserve to feel or be happy!"? Did you experience any of these "bubble bursting" thoughts? If so, that is the past trying to rear its ugly head into the present moment. Remember ego? A part of you might see yourself or want yourself to be deserving, but ego comes into play and says, "Let me handle this!" Unfortunately, ego is still locked in the past mode and is seeking retribution. For SWEET ACCEPTANCE to occur, ego has to let go of the past and basically say, "Whatever!"

SWEET ACCEPTANCE is the decision to forgive, forget and move on from what has happened in the past and create a new currently reality. Your current reality is not who you are as a by-product of your past. You can change it! As soon as you realize and accept you can change things and are not crystallized in the past, or because of what happened to you in the past, you are in the acceptance mode. You are able to see yourself separate from the circumstances/experiences that have happened to you – you become an observing looking in!

Sweet acceptance is the most liberating experience that anyone with an addiction will ever feel. The degree of self-efficacy, freedom and autonomy you feel encompasses you with the most incredible high – high on life rather than high on momentary quick fixes that alcohol, substances and chemicals provide. If you can just shift your mindset into the sweet acceptance mode, even if for 20-30 seconds at a time sporadically throughout the day, you will start to change and re-create the neuropathways in your brain. Your thoughts have the ability to change things/matter! And that is what "matters" most here!

I will often hear people mumble and complain that I don't believe in this stuff – the ability to change things. Well, I ask them five things in sequence:

1) Are you brain dead? I might get a sarcastic response like, "Yeah I'm fried!" After further discussion, ego kicks in and they will assert they can think for themselves and make decisions. After all, many suffering from addictions will have their egos kick in and say stuff like, "I don't need any help!", "I don't have an addiction!", or "I can quit any time I want!" They believe they have everything under control.

2) How good/great is the life you are living currently? This is the question which usually precipitates complaining and grumbling. Funny, once you get them to start discussing how

74

bad things are, their ball gathers and gains momentum for more negativity!

3) Would you say you have happy/positive thoughts throughout most of the day? Most would assert that when they actually start becoming conscious (moment to moment awareness) of their thoughts, the majority of their thoughts are connected to negativity, worry, stress, anger and anxiety.

4) So, if you are not brain dead (meaning you can control what you think about) and you feel miserable all of the time, why is it that you choose miserable thoughts as well as use alcohol, drugs or whatever to try and make you feel better? After all, you did say you are in control? The key here is to examine the reasons that negative thinking exists and is allowed to flourish. After all, where thoughts go, energy flows. If you are thinking negative thoughts, then you are going to flow negative energy. More negative thoughts, more negative energy...it is that simple! So, what are you getting out of thinking and feeling negative? Perhaps this is an excuse to continually play the victim role? In addictions, the concept "enabler" is often heard in reference to people around addicts – individuals who allow them to continue their use. In some cases, enablers actually prefer the individual to remain addicted or with a mental health disorder, as this allows them control over them! Interestingly, you have to *allow* someone permission to enable you. Furthermore, you first must enable yourself! Henceforth, the negative thoughts many people hold onto serve a purpose – to enable oneself for feeling bad!

5) So would you say then there is perhaps a relationship between your negative thinking which cause your bad feelings which lead you to feel worse off? If so, then if thinking negative can make you feel bad, then just maybe thinking good thoughts would make you feel good, you think? After all, bad/negative thoughts are not making you feel good! The purpose here to teach people the role they play in their thinking in terms of the cause-effect relationship which keeps occurring. Your mind is like a blank canvas. Your thoughts are the variety of paint colours that you can choose from. When you splatter these thoughts on the mind, you get feelings. When the artwork for that specific mind-matter is created, what type of painting do you get? Do you get a refreshing, happy, optimistic painting full of like, perhaps a Picasso? Maybe you go the other way and get a more sinister, darker feeling print like a van Gogh? You see, since you are the artist/creator of your feelings, the choice is always yours!

It really is this simple! When you get caught up in a continuum of negative thinking, things begin to flow continually like the following flow chart, which is more characteristic of someone with an addiction, mental health disorder and/or concurrent disorder:

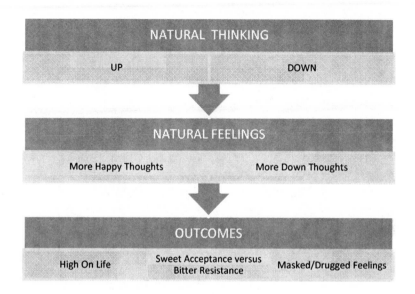

Generally speaking there is no in between or neutral in terms of your natural feeling. You either feel good/bad or up/down. When you hear someone refer to them self as feeling "okay", then they are still in a more positive frame of mind versus a negative one. Even when they say, "It could be better!", they are still feeling good at some unconscious level, or shifting their thinking to a positive vibration, or they would have cited something like, "It keeps getting worse!". Interestingly, the spoken word holds a lot of power. When you speak something out loud, you are giving it existence as well as power in your life. SO ALWAYS SPEAK POSITIVE WORDS ABOUT YOURSELF AND OTHERS!

Most people have their "natural feeling" state. They either feel good or they feel not so good or bad. So the natural state is either positive or negative. When you are feeling good, you are going to continue to draw more good feelings to yourself. You know when you are feeling super good because there is a "butterfly like" feeling in the pit of your stomach – they are flying onward and upward. When you are feeling not so good about yourself, you may feel these same butterflies in the pit of your tummy but they feel grounded as their wings are too heavy – you feel like life in that moment is a downer. When you focus on those types of feelings, you are prone to bring more downward feelings into your conscious which creates a downward spiral. The wings of the butterflies get snipped!

When you continue to produce "up" and happy feelings, you soar and feel good. There is a spring in your psychological walk, literally and figuratively. You continue to draw more feelings of peace, joy, love and contentment which give you a natural high. In fact, positive, healthy endorphins are released in the body. You are high on life!

Conversely, when you feel down you draw more of those feelings of "downers" to you. In bitter resistance people do their best to resist the "down feelings" and the way they go about it is through masking the feelings which shut down the thoughts. They are in essence reversing the process. Of course this doesn't really work other than creating a band aid or masked temporary solution. They will continue to repeat this process leading them to have problems with substance abuse and addictions.

When people who do not have addictions and are able to control their thought process by monitoring them and making rational decisions for responding, you might say they are operating from a platform of sweet acceptance. Even when things are out of their control, there is some kind of acceptance. Just to add...for those reading about addictions for the first time, this famous prayer can be found on many walls, refrigerators, car visors, book marks, wallets, etc. Many individuals with mental health disorders, as well as those individuals who stress easily carry this reminder:

THE SERENITY PRAYER
God grant me the serenity
to *accept* the things I cannot change;
courage to change the things I can;
and *wisdom* to know the difference.

> **Living one day at a time;**
> **Enjoying one moment at a time;**
> ***Accepting*** **hardships as the pathway to peace;**
> **Taking, as He did, this sinful world**
> **as it is, not as I would have it;**
> **Trusting that He will make all things right**
> **if I _surrender_ to His Will;**
> **That I may be reasonably happy in this life**
> **and supremely happy with Him**
> **Forever in the next.**
> **Amen.**
> **~Reinhold Niebuhr**

I underlined what I consider to be the key words associated with this prayer for individuals trying to maintain not only control in their lives, but establishing harmony in all areas. Most people only use the first paragraph of this prayer as a daily reminder. I included the entire prayer because it was intended to be effective in its entirety. I also wanted to include both paragraphs as the word "accept(ing)" appears twice. What is sweet acceptance about? ACCEPTING!

I also underlined the words "wisdom" and "surrender" as both words are extremely important in the process of sweet acceptance. The mantra for so many individuals with addictions is "Let go and let God!" You see, the one who is truly "wise" understands that you can't change the past, so it's important to just accept what has happened, as you only have control over the here and now. With that said, when you "surrender", what you are doing is surrendering what was or what might have been for life – living in the present moment!

So, for positive change to be made and sweet acceptance to occur in an individual's life, the transition would look something like this:

ACCEPTING what happened in the past	SURRENDERING thoughts/emotions tied to the past	SWEET ACCEPTANCE- -Living in and for the present moment

When you get to a position of sweet acceptance in your life I believe you achieve a sense of harmony or harmonic living. Things just kind of go together. In my lectures, seminars and support groups I tend to shy away from using the word or term "balance". The reason I don't like to use "balance" when discussing living is because living connotes life, energy, enjoying life. Balance on the other hand equates with equality or some sort of static position where all things are held constant or equal. In anyone's life, nothing will ever be in balance all at the same time! For example, when you consider a person's complete life, you take into account the following: Psychological well-being, physical health, social life, romantic life, personal wealth/career, etc. Good luck trying to bring these all into balance simultaneously! Instead, you should look at bringing them into "harmony", a way that they can all interact and flourish together rather than antagonizing one another. This is living life in harmony. For many individuals with addictions and mental health problems, they become so obsessed or concerned with keeping everything in balance and making the puzzle pieces fit that it causes them greater angst which leads to greater dysfunction.

Remember how you made your list of things you didn't want as well as the list of things you wanted? Okay, now is the time to set intentions. With intentions words have the power to fix or destroy, heal or hurt, or bring happiness or sadness. Now you are to make your lists more specific as the first time out I wanted you to get a feel for this exercise and explore at a general level. Now comes the "feeling" part. Below I want you to make lists in the following columns and be as thorough as possible.

I DON'T WANT TO ALWAYS FEEL....!	Experiencing this feeling makes me feel? I don't like this because...

The goal is to get your unwanted feelings on paper. Get what you despise feeling the most written on paper and then beside it write why you don't like feeling that feeling. Of course no one wants to feel depressed for the obvious reason, but the reason you are doing this is to describe the feelings as an observer, kind of like being on the outside looking in and being in touch with the feeling intellectually rather than an observer. This exercise teaches people to be more objective with the thoughts leading to their feelings instead of just being subjective – a perceived emoter of doom and gloom!

Okay now I want you to study your list and write out the opposite for every feeling in the left column of the chart you just completed and list the opposites in the right hand column below. In the right hand column, explain how each one of these positive, opposite feelings would make you feel:

THE FEELINGS I MOST WANT!	Experiencing this feeling would make me feel so...

Did you really get in touch with how the "feeling" would make you feel? The goal here is to really feel the new feeling! You see, you are an expert at feeling the old negative feeling because you have done it so many times. When you start to experience new feelings and how they "feel" you begin to create a shift. The goal here is to fit into a new feeling gradually by trying it on for size and customizing the positive feeling to replace the negative feelings. They say that positive feelings vibrate at higher energy frequencies than negative feelings! Over time the good will start to drown out the bad until the bad feelings become no more than an occasional flicker. The goal here is to create a major "feeling shift". This brings about sweet acceptance.

> When we are no longer able to change a situation, we are challenged to change ourselves.
> ~Victor Frankl

Now that you know how experiencing that feeling would make you feel, it is time for you to set intentions related to keeping and maintaining whatever changes you are seeking in your life: sobriety, breaking bad habits, creating good habits, improving your self-esteem, or chasing after whatever dreams and goals you have always had on the back burner.

The following is another present moment exercise. I want you to focus on what you really, really want right here, right now if you could have it. In the mental health world and addictions world, the concept of "the magic wish" is often asked by counsellors. "If you could have one magic wish come true right this moment, what would it be?" Well, imagine the genie can grant you countless wishes as there is no cap to what you want. The goal here is to set intentions in a positive, meaningful manner.

INTENTION	FEELING INSPIRED BY INTENTION
Right now, I intend to have...	This will make me feel...
In this present moment, my intention is...	Because of this I feel...
Right this moment I intend to be...	With this comes the feeling of...

The goal here is more the feeling than the intention. The intention is used to generate the feeling, but really getting into the feeling gets you to the place of getting the intentions you set for yourself. This is a great exercise as what it does when done for at least 21-28 days straight is begin to recreate new neuropathways in the brain. Older, habit formed feelings became engrained in the brain the multiple toboggans going down the same snow-covered hill which eventually makes the pathway thick, polished ice making it easier/quicker to descend.

The toboggan fits inside as if custom made for it. Thoughts are the same way, which lead to feelings. Intense feelings repeated over time also create these slippery slopes for thoughts to jump into and create instant feelings. These exercises are creating new pathways for your thoughts and feelings to slide down...better custom made pathways!

The completed exercises will bring you to the eventual point of sweet acceptance. The goal is to whittle the negative thoughts that lead to the negative feelings until they are minimized while the positive thoughts leading to optimal feelings are maximized. Once you are able to tip the balance to 51% on the positive side, then the positive feelings will continue to grow and up the percentage!

In the end, the statements of intention leading to positive intense feelings would read something like the following examples:

1) I intend to forgive others for any past wrongs they may have done to me. By forgiving them I am relieving the stress and burdens of carrying this weight around with me. I feel so light and relieved that these burdens are gone. I feel complete peace and joy. This makes me feel very happy. Right now I am the happiest I have ever been and this feels so great! Since this feeling is so amazing, I choose this feeling of happiness!

2) I intend to forgive myself for any bad things I may have thought or done to others or myself. I accept the past is the past and I can't change it. I know with confidence I can only change me. This feeling of confidence is liberating and powerful. I am in control of my life right now and I choose greater feelings of freedom, peace and happiness!

3) I intend to leave the past behind and recognize I only have control over the present moment. In this present moment I choose to love myself and others as this is the most powerful experience there is. Since love is unconditional, I accept myself and others for how they are. This feeling of love places me in control to feel even greater feelings of love. This makes me extremely happy!

These are just a few examples for how positive intentions based on feelings (getting into the feeling moment) will help you reach a point of complete sweet acceptance. As I stated before the goal is to write out these intentions each and every day, at least once in the morning and once again at night before bed as that is when the mind is most receptive to encoding/embedding these intentions.

Some people confuse acceptance with apathy, but there's all the difference in the world. Apathy fails to distinguish between what can and what cannot be helped; acceptance makes that distinction. Apathy paralyzes the will-to-action; acceptance frees it by relieving it of impossible burdens.

~ Arthur Gordon

SECTION TWO

APPLYING SPIRITUALISM AND THE LAW OF ATTRACTION FOR OVERCOMING ADDICTION, VICES, BAD HABITS AND FOR A NEW WAY OF THINKING POSITIVELY

CHAPTER FIVE:

SPIRITUAL EMPTINESS

"The Divine Spirit does not reside in any except
the joyful heart."

The Talmud Quotes

When most people read or hear about spiritualism or the Law of Attraction they associate the concept with something bigger than themselves and the world they live in, at least the world they can perceive with their own eyes. When you are a believer in God, Jesus, Buddha, The Divine, the Universal Mind, etc., there is a greater process at work in the Universe, whether it be outside of oneself or within oneself. The "spiritual" component of the *bio-psycho-socio-spiritual* process which I have discussed in this book is just as important as the other components, maybe more! The spiritual component often times gets the least amount of attention, but has the greatest ability to create lasting change as most underlying problems exist within in it!

When treating addiction, vices, bad habits and/or improving the mindset for creating good habits, the first place to start is within oneself. Most people with addictions or feeling a sense of "lack" in their lives often report a sense of emptiness. Do you know what this "emptiness" is? It is *spiritual* emptiness!

Spiritual emptiness is getting to the place of a spiritual "bottoming out" where there is nothing left to hang onto within one's "self". Remember, bitter resistance is all about holding onto the bad stuff—memories, perceptions and evils of wrongs done to you. You hold onto things as if they are a part of you, as if they are required to keep you running. In fact, they keep you running from your true essence, the spiritual you and the connection you have to your Higher Power...God or the Universe! When you operate from this mindset, you are basically "keeping on keeping on" in the wrong direction. What does this do? It creates a malnourished spirit, causing it to be disconnected, weak and, dare I say, poor?

I once heard someone refer to this impoverished and lacking spirit as being "bankrupt". I would say that is the best way to define this spirit state. Holding onto bitterness and resisting change for the better will cause the spirit to feel bankrupted.

In order to accept this part of the healing process, the individual needs to do three things:

1) **Admit that they need help.**
2) **Identify their weak spots or triggers which bring them down.**
3) **Surrender to a Higher Power for help as well as other positive sources of help outside of themselves.**

---

1) Admitting you need help outside of yourself.

The first part of the problem is that many individuals believe they are "okay" or that they have everything under control. They believe they can manage it from the inside out which is what is causing them their problems in the first place. The self is being mismanaged by the self!

Remember addiction and even bad habits are the results of doing things the same way and getting the same outcome. For addiction, the individual engages in the same destructive behaviour hoping for or expecting a different outcome.

Insanity is doing the same thing over and over again and expecting different results.

~Albert Einstein

Most people are afraid to admit their shortcomings and weaknesses because they don't want to appear inferior to others. So many people are living their lives that continue to fall apart every day from the inside out. Often times those on the outside do not even know this person is crumbling. Conversely, many people on the outside looking in recognize this individual has certain problems and with the proper help could actually change their lives for the better. They refuse to change, especially at the encouragement or insistence of loved ones because that would place them in a place of perceived inferiority thus making those around them appear to be superior to them. Does this make sense? People would rather drown in their addictions and bad habits and irrationally believe they are in control versus agreeing to go along with the advice of significant others who have their best interests in mind—following their advice would actually help them attain positive and productive control over their life, perhaps for the first time in a long time!

Ironically it is those who admit their weaknesses and admit they need help that places them in a place of superiority—they learn what true control entails. Superiority in life comes from knowing that help is always available and that with a simple request, "Help is on the way!" In order to master one's own life one has to realise they can't do it alone. Even the most powerful, successful and wealthiest people in the world ask for help as they delegate authority. Remember earlier in the book I asserted that no man/woman is an island, meant to live life alone without supports. It is this insistence based on ego that one must do everything alone which causes their spirit to eventually become bankrupt. The more one tries to endeavour in their quest for doing it "their way" which causes them madness down the path of repeated failures, the more inclined they are to engage in substance use/abuse to mask the feelings of failure. The only one who is measuring and judging their perceived failures is them alone

I would like to use the example of the Johari Window to explain what happens in this state of resistance before the individual with the substance abuse problem, habit or addiction admits they need help. The Johari Window was developed to demonstrate people's dysfunctional or mental instability by Joseph Luft and Harry Ingham in 1955. The process of using the Johari Window is an excellent tool for individuals to learn about themselves in support groups and/or education settings. Please look at the diagram of the Johari Window.

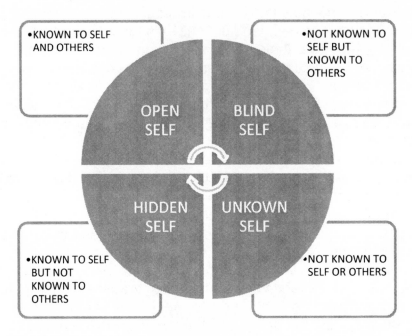

As you can see, the OPEN SELF is seen by everyone. You don't try to hide anything. What you see is what you get! In the HIDDEN SELF you do things that are known only to you and you are able to keep things under wraps so to speak. In the BLIND SELF, there are things you do that you are unaware of that others are aware of. And in the UNKNOWN SELF, you do things that are unknown to others as well as yourself, at least consciously.

When it comes to habits, addictions and some mental health disorders, the HIDDEN SELF usually rules in the beginning or outset of most substance use/abuse. The individual who engages in secret activities is usually able to keep their habit which leads to an addiction under lock and key. They are able to control the use, situation and circumstances of use. Most people, even those closest to them have no idea that things may be growing out of control for the user.

When things get progressively worse and bad habits or addiction kicks in, then the individual moves more into OPEN SELF where they are less discreet with their use and abuse of the substance. In fact, many make their substance abuse problem appear in total control as well as incorporating publicly as part of their persons or lifestyle. As the use/abuse gets worse, those closest to them begin to identify red flags and may even bring them to the attention of the user. Of course they downplay it!

When the use and abuse escalates into an out of control habit or addiction, then the BLIND SELF becomes more prevalent. This is when the substance user begins lacking control and doing things they are unaware of or cross the line of social acceptance. This is when bitter resistance kicks in and they become in denial of their problem. This is also the point individuals close to them are most likely to be more vocal and encourage them to seek outside help. The user resists them. The more they push the user to get help the more the user resists as they feel others are trying to place them in a position of inferiority.

It is at this phase in the process that the user decides if their ego will rule and they will continue on their downward spiral, or if they will admit that they need help.

---

2) Identifying the weak spots or triggers which bring you down.

In this next phase individuals need to identify their triggers—weaknesses or weakest links in their lives which lead them to use and abuse substances. The secret to any success in life is identifying our weaknesses and doing whatever we can to overcome them. Often times your best source for identification is not yourself, as you are in denial, rather those outside of you who are offering their "two cents" which is really a treasure chest of wealth in terms of concern for your wellbeing and getting you moving in the right direction.

In the Johari Window, you are often missing the truths for what is going on in your hidden areas...your blind spots. Missing what is going on in blind spots is often a recipe for accidents to occur. Blind spots in the hidden self might best be considered as an "ignorant spot" where one chooses to ignore that area of their life because they are afraid of what they might really see or it is blocked from the conscious mind because the bitter resistance harboured in the unconscious is held onto by the unconscious mind because it feels the need to keep it alive. Furthermore, the unconscious mind is wired to respond and react to certain triggers that are wired in.

One of the biggest triggers for most individuals trapped in bitter resistance is low self-esteem. When you are lacking in certain areas of your life, emotionally, mentally and/or psychologically you look to compensate for this lack. Unfortunately, the "feelings" created from this lack are often momentary, and the individual is triggered by these "feelings of lack" to engage in some quick fix or momentary solution to relieve their negative feelings or lack and disparity.

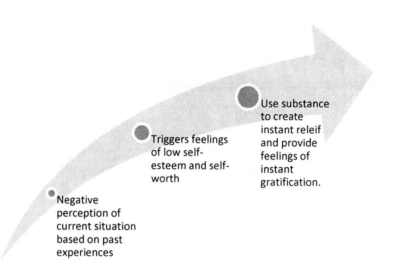

Use substance to create instant releif and provide feelings of instant gratification.

Triggers feelings of low self-esteem and self-worth

Negative perception of current situation based on past experiences

---

3) Surrendering to a Higher Power for help as well as other positive sources of help outside of yourself.

In the final phase individuals have to learn to surrender or relinquish whatever it is they are holding onto which is pulling them down. You've already accepted that you need help outside of yourself. You've realized that you have certain triggers which cause you to stumble or fall and you've accepted the constructive criticism others have offered you. So now comes the third part which some consider the most difficult – letting go!

Even though people know they are their own worst enemies at this point as their faulty thinking has gotten them on the detrimental path they are on, giving up control and trusting in others and God/the Universal Mind is the hardest thing they may ever have to do in their lives. I have found that in talking to clients and individuals in recovery, many of them tell me this is so hard because in the past they have been let down and they believe they will be let down by others, even God again! One of the problems so many humans face is that they have been let down, felt rejected or even have been rejected by their biological fathers. Since God is the "Father of creation" many use their own fathers to form opinions for what "God the Father must be like. Unfortunately those who have been hurt by their fathers feel they can't trust God because He too will let them down. So many choose to live their hurt and angst even though they admit they have a problem and realize they have triggers and know they have to stop them. When they get to the point of surrender, bitter resistance from past wrongs resurface and the idea of surrender just becomes too big of a risk for them. What can they do?

In order for God/the Universal Mind, a greater power or fellow humans to help, you first have to surrender. True surrender means trusting, which I know is probably the hardest thing you will ever be asked to do again. Surrender also means letting go of the past. To truly surrender you have to forgive the past; what others have done to you, what others didn't do for you, as well as what you have done to yourself.

Two things have to happen for true surrender to occur. First, you have to admit that you need help. Second, you have to admit that this help must come from outside of you. Surrender is all about an "outstretched arms" attitude...I NEED HELP!

To summarize this entire 3-phase process:

1) I admit that I need help! I continually do the same things and these things bring me the same negative results!

2) I am lacking something in my life, which causes me to react to unconscious triggers, which sets me up for failure!

3) I surrender! I am sorry for holding onto grudges and unforgiving feelings towards others as well as myself. Whether it is God/the Universal Mind or someone reliable, I will trust them to help me find my way toward a positive outcome!

These three steps are all set as intentions. Just saying them is a start. Writing them out repeatedly is even better! You begin to teach and retrain the mind a new way of thinking.

EXERCISE ONE

By now this has probably been allowed to absorb into your mind and you have a pretty good understanding for what it means. The goal now will be to help you work through the 3 phases and get your mind open and alert to change before moving on.

PART ONE

"I admit that I need help! I continually do the same things and these things bring me the same negative results!" SAY THIS OUT LOUD AND FEELING IT...MEAN IT!

Now comes the part where you are going to have let down your critical ego and do the following:

Brainstorm and write out a list of things in your life where you believe you need the most help. There are areas where you tried to change things on your own but it doesn't seem to work. (You are applying old methods to try to create new outcomes.) Next, and this is where you really have to let go of your ego, invite two or three of your closest acquaintances to make similar lists about you where they believe you need the most help. These should be people who are clean and sober, grounded in good decision making, and ones you trust wholeheartedly!

PART TWO

"I am lacking something in my life which causes me to react to unconscious triggers which set me up for failure!"

Make a list of situations or things in your life which repeatedly set you off. These would be people, things and situations that you are around where you feel you lose control and they cause you to fall into your bad habits, substance use/abuse, or send you on a negative mental spiral. These are your triggers! Now you need to identify, 1) why do you enjoy or place yourself around these triggers, and 2) what do these people, places and situations usually do for you? Do they make you bitter? Do they make you angrier? Do they cause you to become depressed? 3) As your feelings kick in, what do you usually do to tame or extinguish your negative feelings? 4) Twenty-four to 48 hours later, do you have regrets about giving into your triggers and then feeling even worse about using or abusing substances to try and negate everything?

The point of trigger identification is three-fold. First the obvious one is to know what your triggers are. Second, you need to know what feelings specific triggers elicit in you. Thirdly, there is some investment tied to the negative feeling surrounding the trigger if it serves to perpetuate bitter resistance. You see, for this last part, it is really important to get into the feeling and dissect it. You continually welcome this feeling as it helps you to re-experience the past. Remember, misery loves company, and when you are in bitter resistance states, your misery is looking for negative feelings to latch onto in order to not only survive but grow!

Complete the following chart and be as specific as possible.

TRIGGERS - People, places & situations that set me off!	FEELING(S) - This is how I feel when triggered.	COST - What does feeling this way accomplish?

Study your lists closely. Once again, I can't emphasize enough that it is really important that you "feel" column three – COSTS!

"I surrender! I am ready to let go!"

How can I surrender my negative and detrimental feelings that I have carried with me for longer than I can remember? First you name it, second identify the cost and then surrender it. Take out a piece of lined paper and then start writing out your feeling with the accompanying cost. For example, your statement may read something like this;

"I feel so angry when my spouse puts me down. When this happens I feel the need to argue to prove my worth. Things always escalate and get out of control! I hate how I feel afterwards. I feel extremely uneasy physically and emotionally. I find that I have to have a couple of drinks to take the edge off. The more I drink, the more emotional I become and I need to drink more." In this statement you see the trigger, feeling and cost. Now, in this situation, what can you do to let go? *"I could ignore my spouse's comments. I could let myself know that the putdowns are not true. I could just walk away. I could get angrier and be more aggressive!"* What happens here are options, both positive and negative. Making a list of the positive and negative options in this scenario might look something like this:

POSITIVE OPTIONS	NEGATIVE OPTIONS
Walk away and keep the peace	Get in their face and argue more
Acknowledge what is said as mistruths	Believe what they are saying is true
Tell my spouse what they are saying is unacceptable	Agree with my spouse by arguing

Anything you list in the "POSITIVE OPTIONS" side are surrenders! You are letting go to be precise. Anything you list on the "NEGATIVE OPTIONS" side are embedded in and based on bitter resistance and you need to work on them. The goal is not only to create positive options to deal with all of your triggers, but also to incorporate them into your thinking process on a daily basis. Remember earlier in the book you made lists of "WHAT I DON'T WANT" and then converted them into lists of "WHAT I DO WANT"? Well you are going to do the same thing here.

Use a list as follows to complete this exercise for each negative option that you have in your response to your trigger list (cost):

I DON'T WANT THIS NEGATIVE FEELING	I WANT TO EXPERIENCE THIS POSITIVE FEELING	I CAN ACCOMPLISH THIS BY... (brainstorm options)

Surrendering in this exercise is based on discipline which means identifying options. Letting go and letting God/the Universal Mind, or seeking outside sources, is really all about disciplining oneself (surrender) which means you know you have to work on something that is going to remove you from the current situation.

Take your list of brainstormed options and explore them. If you have a problem with addiction and/or mental health issues, it would be best to do this with a counselor or someone you can trust. It is now important to treat this aspect of the exercise like a vacation you know you want to go on. When you book a vacation, you visit the travel agent and they provide you with the most efficient and cost-effective method for travelling. You surrender your trust to them believing they know best. At this point you need to be able to turn it over to God/the Universal Mind and/or counselors, or if you are not addicted or possess a mental health problem to implement methods to get your positive brainstormed options working in your life in the present moment. I believe three minds are better all the way around! Mind #1 = God/the Universal Mind. Tap into the power of meditation/prayer. Mind #2 = Counselor or someone close to you that you trust for feedback. Mind #3 = Your own mind. In the end, you have to understand that whatever is going to work will rely mostly on your mental discipline and ability to carry things out as planned. The key thing is to never give up!

CHAPTER SIX:

ASKING FOR HELP!

"If you learn from your suffering, and really come to understand the lesson you were taught, you might be able to help someone else
who's now in the phase you may have just completed. Maybe that's what it's all about after all..."

Anonymous

There is no living human being who at some point in their life is not going to know what grief feels like firsthand. For some, it is more intense and prolonging than it is forever.

There is a season for mourning (grieving) and then there is a return to happiness. People are spiritual beings and the spirit was designed to be full of joyfulness and peace. People who focus on grief and only grief will only bring more grief into their lives.

Whether you believe in God/the Universal Mind or not, comforting is always available for those who seek it. There is no way anyone should or has to go through life without getting support from someone or something outside of themselves. Remember when you admit that you need help and are willing to surrender you are saying, "I need help, I can't do this myself and I need something from outside of me to come into my life and provide me positive comfort!"

You see, many who mourn seek comfort from vices and substances outside of them, the wrong kind of comfort! They process and believe that comfort can be structured and/or contained based on their own terms. Their terms are dysfunctional and based on bitter resistance. And the comfort they seek is often momentary...a bandage solution. Individuals suffering from addiction or bad vices need to acknowledge that comfort has to come from outside of them, and something other than what they have used to that point which has served as nothing more than a diversion needs to be experienced.

Mourning is normal when one has experienced some major loss in their life. And this mourning does have a season. It is when this mourning becomes wallowing in grief that it starts to become a problem. You see, when you start to wallow in grief, you let the grief begin to control you. Furthermore, when grief begins to control you, you start to get into a passive, more victim-like mindset of, "Why me? Why do things like this have to happen to me?" This mindset places you in a greater position of weakness and victimisation. What you start to experience is a sense of learned helplessness. The longer you shift into this mindset the more likely you are to become it and act according to it. You start to view as being unfair and that you have no control over things so it is easy to withdraw and try to seek solace and comfort in being a "victim"! After all, some people enjoy the comfort they get initially from being a victim. This occurrence gets them attention they otherwise would not have received. After a while this attention provides a sense of acceptance and comfort. After a while those giving the comfort usually withdraw their attention because life goes on and the individual feels further victimised as they feel rejected by the comforters. The comforters did their best to help and comfort in the season of mourning, however they realize life goes and so should you!

Then there are those who provide comfort which causes individuals to become enabled. The comforter likes to be a caregiver and the comforted enjoys being taken care of. This only instigates and facilitates feelings of co-dependency and a greater cycle of enabling. The comforter gets their feelings of importance by acting as a "caregiver" and the comforted feels their role in life is to be the "victim". What this causes and leads to is tremendous levels of frustration for both of them which leads to a very bad dysfunctional relationship. This is often seen in alcoholic relationships as well as Munchausen Syndrome and Munchausen by Proxy Syndrome.

Munchausen Syndrome: A psychiatric disorder where one feigns an illness to draw and receive attention/sympathy for themselves.

Munchausen by Proxy Syndrome: This where caregivers/loved ones deliberately create or exaggerate physical and/or mental health symptoms in others to have control over them.

In either version of Munchausen syndromes, attention is the primary concern where there is some qualifying role of victimisation created. No doubt, this only perpetuates a greater sense of victimisation as well as co-dependency.

The longer one "mourns", which leads to a sense of entitled prolonged victimisation, the more likely psychological and mental health problems are likely to become prevalent.

CYCLE OF FEELING VICTIMISED

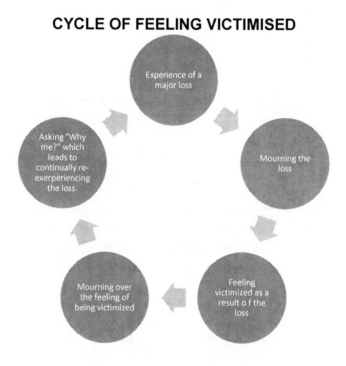

When you study the Cycle of Feeling Victimised diagram, you can see how reliving the same experience over and over will perpetuate greater feelings of being the victim. Perhaps the strongest component of this negative cycle is the "Why me?" part where you seek answers that start with "Why?"

"Why" questions usually do not have answers to them because no one can really give you an answer people who feel victimised are satisfied with. Furthermore, questions that start with "Why" are often set up to be argumentative. When bad things happen to good people, this is oftentimes when people want to know "why". And the answer truly is "Only God knows!" When people ask God/the Universal Mind these questions beginning with "why" and do not get the answer they are looking for, they then believe God has let them down or they can't trust God. This is one of the reasons some people shy away from 12-step groups and support groups that involve the concept of a Higher Power. They felt let down once or thrice and they do not want to go there again.

"Why" questions will only cause you to analyze things to death. You will get caught up in self-induced games of mental/emotional gymnastics where you wind up feeling like a mental pretzel. That is not good! Furthermore, many people who seek "why's" oftentimes do not really want reasoning and/or explanations as much as they want to argue. When individuals are caught up in this victimisation cycle, they can't get their minds off faulty, destructive thought patterns – why do bad things happen to good people? Instead, they need to look at the question more productively and positively which would bring them out of their mourning season. They could be asking the question, "What do good people do when bad things happen to them – how do they overcome?"

As spiritual beings and creations of God/the Universal Mind, the Divine source, we were created to be people who look for the best that make us better rather than people who become bitter over time. The more you come bitter, the more you become resistant to any sort of change that is out of the realm of bitterness. The bitter taste in one's mouth grows more permanent that anything sweet that passes one's lips tastes bitter, or they believe will turn bitter because "Bad things always happen to them."

The second component of bitterness is guilt. Remember, individuals who develop bitter resistance do so because they feel victimised and try to make sense of things according to their faulty logic. The more you analyze things the more you shift between victimisation and blame. When you run out of people to blame, you start to point the finger at yourself. You begin to blame yourself because you believe you could have done something differently or prevented it. This faulty thinking begins to perpetuate the qualities of omniscience (all knowing) and omnipotence (all powerful), traits that God/the Universal Mind possesses, within the individual. They start to play "God" in their minds believing they could have created a different outcome. "Could of, should of, would have..." becomes their mantra. This creates overwhelming feelings of guilt as they believe they were great failures. For some, this only reaffirms their sense of "helplessness". They believe they are impotent in the real world and this causes them to become anxious living in fear. To mask these inferior feelings they drink or drug to mask their perceived sense of powerlessness.

Some individuals believe the tragic experience occurred because they are being punished by God/the Universal Mind for something they did. They wallow in a mindset of things they have done wrong in the past (sins) and believe this is God's way of punishing them. From this, they believe they could never surrender to God as they believe they are not worthy to take their concerns to God/the Universal Mind – after all they believe God/the Universal Mind punished them and they could never be right with the Divine! Guilt only produces greater feelings of shame, fear and mourning. Guilt will always perpetuate the blaming game which always produces a sense of victimisation.

The key component of mourning is eventually letting go. Letting go and letting God/the Universal Mind is the way to overcome feelings of victimisation!

LET GO AND LET GOD!

When you carry your grief around and allow it to harden in your life, you, in essence, become selfish. This selfishness affects three sectors: God/the Universal Mind, others and yourself!

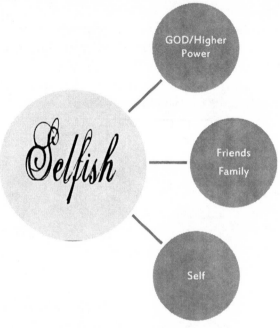

SELF RELATIONSHIP

Firstly, if you believe in God, the Divine or a Higher Power, then you have been given a gift of life. Life was meant to be enjoyed and "lived". When you continually mourn, you deny yourself this gift of life and living. This also denies others from enjoying you!

When you continually mourn and feel that you are a victim, you push others away as well as withdraw from them. People, especially family and friends need you and want you in their lives. You deny them of you!

Finally, continual mourning becomes a selfish act directed at yourself. If you can detach yourself from you for a moment and see you as continual victim, miserable and participating in self-destructive behaviours, then you know you are doing wrong to yourself. You are existing, enduring life on your own negative terms and just getting by. Life was made to enjoy and live!

Truly embracing help and surrendering means accepting whatever God/the Universal Mind, and others are sending your way. To deny the comfort of the Higher Power and others keeps you from evolving and healing. With comfort you continually operate on a self-destructive ego focussed on blame, victimisation and selfishness.

EXERCISE TWO

How you are handling 3 negative qualities that may be occurring in your life: **MOURNING, BLAMING** and **WITHDRAWING/GUILT**. The key is to tap into these 3 areas that are continually perpetuating bitter resistance. You will need paper and a pen to complete this exercise.

Take a moment to collect your thoughts before jumping into this exercise. The goal is to bring those feelings that are bubbling below the surface that you have been unable to name, identify and accept. Once you are able to do this, you can purge them, release them and receive the "comfort" that you need.

PART ONE - MOURNING

Over the next couple of days write out in detail as if journaling those events in your life that have had a strong emotional impact (ones that really caused you to grieve). After writing them out, evaluate each one of them and ask yourself, "Am I still grieving this or have I accepted it and moved on?" The proof will be in the pudding so to speak. You will know if you are still mourning it if it causes you to become extremely emotional over it. If and when you become extremely emotional over something that has happened in the past, you are to move onto PART TWO.

PART TWO - BLAMING

Using the event which has triggered in you intense feelings/emotions as if it was still happening in your present moment, ask yourself if you are affixing blame to someone, something or God/the Universal Mind in this situation. Really get in touch with the emotions surrounding "blaming". If you are blaming, then it means that you haven't truly forgiven yourself, others or the Divine for what happened. So, if you are blaming, write out statements that begin with, "I am blaming so and so for this event..." Then explain by writing out why you are blaming them for the event. After you have been honest with yourself and others/God (writing it out as if they were there listening), move onto PART THREE.

PART THREE - WITHDRAWING/GUILT

Your blaming has led you over time to withdraw from addressing the feelings surrounding a situation from the past that was never dealt with and resolved. Most likely, you have tried to repress those feelings which arise when situations perceived as being similar to that past event happen. Those same feelings come up and cause you to feel uneasy, most likely leading you to feel guilty and disgusted with yourself over how you feel. If you use/abuse substances or engage in bad habits, this "event" is most likely triggering you to use.

Write out, in as much detail as possible, expressing your feelings that you forgive others, yourself and God/the Universal Mind for what happened. Really get into the feeling aspect. You need not beat yourself over the head asking for forgiveness a zillion times. All you have to do is ask for forgiveness once saying you are sorry. This is just for you and if you are a believer in the Divine, a Higher Power or God, then it is between you and Them as well.

Once you have completed this, you are ready to move on to **COMFORT!**

ACCEPTING COMFORT

Whether you have apologized in person or on paper, you are sorry for what you have done. When you go before God/the Universal Mind and ask for forgiveness, you are immediately forgiven, slate wiped clean and ready to live!

In order to accept comfort (forgiveness) which is readily available to you, you have to pull your mind out of the past, as that aspect of your life has now been resolved. By reliving it, will not change it. Re-experiencing the emotions is not a good penance and will not earn you brownie points with God, others or yourself!

I believe if you feel the need to go and apologize to someone in person, first apologise to yourself for what you have done as well as God/the Universal Mind. This way if you do approach someone you have wronged and they do not receive your forgiveness, you already know that you have been forgiven in advance and their lack of forgiveness cannot bring you down.

If you need to really get it off your chest, then go share it with a counsellor. This is another example of accepting comfort, even if it is having someone listen to you. You should only do this once as you have been forgiven, accepted forgiveness and dispelled the guilt. If you continually talk about it, then you are re-accepting guilt and blame.

CHAPTER SEVEN:

BECOMING CALM, COOL AND COLLECTED!

"The most intense conflicts, if overcome, leave behind a sense of security and calm that is not easily disturbed. It is just these intense conflicts and their conflagration which are needed to produce valuable and lasting results."

Carl Jung

Let me ask you this question: Who appears to be more in control when faced with pressure—the individual who keeps their cool and remains as calm as possible while they think things through, or the person who blows their cool and explodes into a fit of rage? If you were hiring a manager to run your company, sports team or family, of these two; the mild mannered/rationale or the time bomb waiting to explode, who would you select? I am sure most of you would select the cool, mild-mannered, rational person because they have it together. They are capable of exploding like the other personality type but they operate from a position of grace under pressure. They seem to have it together and come off as more intelligent, in control and trustworthy—they don't let their emotions rule. When people are ruled by their emotions they often are unable to think rationally thus making poor decisions. Therefore, most would prefer stability, integrity, calmness and patience in a leader. And if you truly wanted a leader who possessed great might then case closed—harnessed might wins over explosive might. That truly harnessed might is meekness!

When it comes to mental health healing and addictions recovery, it is all about emotional stability—remaining calm and in control! What are some of the qualities of individuals who are "calm/control" types who prevent them from being prone to, or falling to addictions? Also, what are the qualities of "calmness" which allow those with addictions, mental health issues or bad habits to recover?

Below is a chart I have created to help you better understand how these certain qualities are tied to "calmness" and how they can lead an individual to fall to bad habits and addiction:

DISTRACTIONS	• Allowing other people's problems/issues to become your own. • Being influenced by outside sources you don't normally accept or succumbing to conformity.
DISCOURAGEMENTS	• Viewing setbacks and problems as failures rather than opportunities for growth/change. • Quitting/withdrawing whenever faced with adversity.
TEMPTATIONS	• Placing yourself in situations where you know you might lose control. • Continuing to associate with the wrong people who place you in bad situations or add no good to your life.

QUALITIES TAKING AWAY A SENSE OF CALM

People who are easily distracted are often times unable to separate themselves from circumstances and other people's problems. They get caught up the whirlwinds of other people's problems and take on their stresses. Before they know it they are infected by the same stresses that have these people's lives out of control. People who become easily distracted get caught up in mob mentality — everyone is doing it so must I? How many teens took up smoking, drugging, drinking and gambling because "everyone" else was doing it? How bad did you need to fit in to be "one of the gang"? Of course you thought you could quit any time you wanted…it was just for fun! Where did that get you?

Individuals who are easily discouraged are more likely to be ruled by their emotions. They are more prone to take things too personally. Often times they magnify or blow a single, isolated incident out of proportion and allow it to be characteristic of their lives — a reflection of their pasts. They immediately shift into the mindsets of; "Same ole story...", or "Here we go again!" and allow their thoughts to focus on past feelings they come to life and they regress. Their minds create thoughts based on past experiences which reincarnate the same feelings from the past. They believe that the past is coming to life in the present...back to the future if you will! Instead of working through the current adversities and problems with the opportunity to grow and learn from them, they often times withdraw or quit all together. For individuals with addictions, these moments become their faulty reasons/excuses for using!

Temptations are those circumstances that involve people, places and things that place you in a position of potentially losing self-control. Throughout this book I have discussed triggers, those people, places, situations, things which are most likely to get an individual into a mindset of want to use/abuse substances. Individuals who lack calmness are more likely to fall to their immature whims which are influenced by these triggers. Moreover, they place themselves in situations where they are more likely to lose control because their egos trick them into believing they are above their triggers. In fact, they place themselves in destructive situations or hang around the "wrong types of people" as they believe they are above and beyond that, or they feel the need to be tested.

The calm can create within themselves a sense of self-control. They know they are the creators of their own fates rather than buying into a "powerful locus of control" which means that their circumstances and choices are dictated outside of them by some powerful other or circumstance. They get that life is all about attitude...how you respond to a situation. Emotionally healthy stable people tend to be more patient and intentional in their decision making process. Their decisions and actions are mighty, no knee jerking or acting fair-weathered where they blow with the directional changes of the wind. They stand steadfast in their beliefs which are derived from seeking wisdom.

Perhaps the greatest attribute of a calm individual is they seek wisdom and information from the best sources. Calm people are teachable, they do not hold onto the notion they know everything. They seek help outside of themselves when in doubt – that is real power and control!

The key to being psychologically mighty and wise is to seek information and insights from those who know more than you do. Those people are those folks who have already traveled down the path to the destination of the mind and heart that you are trying to get to. Wise people know how to do 3 things; 1) Avoid unnecessary distractions, 2) Identify potential discouragements as opportunities for wisdom and improvement, and 3) Avoid temptations, identifying their triggers beforehand or at the point where they can cause harm.

Now I want you to examine the chart below to see controlling the negative factors from the previous chart leads one to finding the calmness they are seeking to find:

| AVOID DISTRACTIONS | •Don't allow other people's problems/issues to become your own.
•Decide what is right from you rather than accepting outside influences that go against your beliefs. |

| INDENTIFY DISCOURAGEMENTS AS OPPORTUNITIES | •Whatever you feel you have failed at in past as present, view as a lesson to get things right which will happen with persistence! |

| AVOID TEMPTATIONS | •Avoid any and all situations/people you know might lead you to slip, backslide or cause your life harm. |

QUALITIES LEADING TO A SENSE OF CALM

These are the tremendous abilities that learning to be clam will offer you. When you allow yourself to become teachable and are willing to accept the things you cannot change, the courage/strength to change the things you can and the smarts to know the difference, then you have truly arrived. You best might be described as – a calm, cool, and collected person who is living a great life, one that you were intended to have!

EXERCISE THREE

In this exercise, you are going to make your own "calm/collected" quality lists for **DISTRACTIONS**, **DISCOURAGEMENTS** and **TEMPTATIONS**.

In the following charts, write out what you currently see as your own in the present moment:

THESE ARE THE BIGGEST AND MOST PREVALENT DISTRACTIONS CURRENTLY IN MY LIFE THAT CAUSE ME DISCOMFORT:
1)
2)
3)
4)
5)
6)
THESE ARE THE MOST CURRENT THINGS THAT HAVE HAPPENED IN THE LAST 6 MONTHS TO 1 YEAR WHICH CONTINUE TO DISCOURAGE ME:
1)
2)
3)
4)
5)
6)
7)

I WOULD CONSIDER THE FOLLOWING TO BE THE BIGGEST TEMPTATIONS (PEOPLE, PLACES, THINGS, SITUATIONS) IN MY LIFE:
1)
2)
3)

4)	
5)	
6)	

Okay, now that you listed the bad and ugly, let's have you make a list of the good! Complete the following, meditating on your answers, brainstorming them to provide adequate solutions:

I CAN REMOVE MY MOST PREVALENT DISTRACTIONS IN MY LIFE THAT CAUSE ME DISCOMFORT BY:
1)
2)
3)
4)
5)
6)

WHAT HAVE I LEARNED OR WHAT CAN I LEARN FROM THOSE THINGS THAT DISCOURAGE ME?:
1)
2)
3)
4)
5)
6)

I CAN USE THESE ESCAPES/WAYS OUT TO THE BIGGEST TEMPTATIONS (PEOPLE, PLACES, THINGS, SITUATIONS) IN MY LIFE WHEN FACED WITH TEMPTATION:
1)
2)
3)

4)	
5)	
6)	

Excellent! I want you to memorize what you wrote in the last 3 lists. Also, I want you to continue to use these three lists as exercises whenever you are faced with adversity. Truly, if it is going to be, then it will be up to you!

One last thing. At this point, if you have not found someone honest, trustworthy and wise to bounce ideas off of, then now is the time for sure. Remember, calmness and collectiveness comes from being teachable and this is the point where you are past the point of surrender and ready/willing to accept whatever help you can get!

CHAPTER EIGHT:

CHOOSING AND PURSUING TO DO WHAT IS RIGHT!

"It is of practical value to learn to like yourself. Since you must spend so much time with yourself, you might as well get some satisfaction out of the relationship."

Norman Vincent Peale

In this chapter, the focus is on embracing the spirit inside of you that yearns for being the best you can be. Choosing and pursuing righteousness is setting your mind toward success!

Human beings are created with spirit...we are spiritual beings. I believe spirituality is comprised of our psychological ability to perceive, conceive and grasp the notion that we are greater than who and what we think we are and how we see ourselves in the mirror. If you study Abraham Maslow's existential theories, at the top of his 5 hierarchy of needs he places self-actualization followed second by esteem needs. Maslow asserted that most human beings are able to attain the bottom three; physical needs, safety needs and loving/belonging needs. Most people subscribed to the notion that if you own a house/apartment (have somewhere to live) and have food on your plate, feel safe and possess some sense of security and then feel loved and reciprocate it, then they've "arrived", after all this is the traditional/typical American dream. Don't get me wrong here as I am not saying that you should not be grateful for having these qualities in your life. In fact, you should express gratitude for this each and every morning you awake. And here is the rub...

Maslow believed only a small percentage make it to the next level in the attainment of esteem needs. Furthermore, he believed that minuscule select few ever attain a level of self-actualization.

For all intents and purposes, the bottom 3 needs are basic and almost givens from the time we are toddlers, children and teens. We will all experiences them to some degree. It is also during this time during early childhood development, 'tween years and especially adolescent years that the seeds for the development of self-esteem are planted. Depending on the social surrounding you are raised in (family, friends, school, etc.) this self-esteem either becomes positive or negative. Self-esteem is the way you perceive yourself and the self-worth you place on yourself. In fact, too many make their self-worth contingent on their current success (what they've accomplished and done lately), what they own and material possessions. After all, this is the "American dream"…owning the most toys. At the end of the day for many who have all of this stuff, they still feel empty inside, like there is something missing, some void that can never be filled. The reason is they equated self-esteem with mere accomplishment and what they own. They feel like there is just something that keeps eluding them, or making them miserable and they feel lacking psychologically and or depressed. By engaging in whatever they are doing and doing "more of it", they believe they can fill this void. So people stop living their lives in moderation and go to extremes hoping to satiate their needs. You can imagine the rest...desensitization, tolerance and addiction!

Good self-esteem comes from placing a positive sense of self-worth on yourself. Individuals are able to feel good about themselves, knowing that self-worth is not contingent on material worth. In fact, I have met so many people who less than those who have more and they are happier in their lives. What then is this "self-esteem" which leads people to eventually transcend to the next level and feel self-actualized (the greatest degree of self-fulfillment—reaching one's full potential)? Perhaps William James one of the greatest psychologists of all time put it, "The most important thing in one's life is to live their life for something more important than their life!" People have the ability to do so much more with their lives, attain higher potential but settle and become complacent. They get stuck on "the American dream".

First of all, you have to look at yourself as being worthy. In the Hollywood movie Wayne's World, the main characters Wayne and Garth are famous for their line, "We're not worthy!" It's just a comedy but how many people walk around saying that to themselves, "We're not worthy...I'm not worthy."? Too many! No matter who you are, where you came from, or what you have, you are worthy! Self-esteem is thinking, feeling, acting and becoming worthy. You are worthy!

In their teen and adult years too many people associate failure in their lives with self-worth. People are taught to believe they are only as good as their last performance. This is a misconception that too many take to heart and before long it becomes at the heart of their belief system.

I believe many have "God-given" dreams as children. There is something they have always wanted to be when they grew up, or something they have always wanted to do. Unfortunately there were those who talked them out of these dreams and told them why it couldn't come to pass. With that said, I believe there is unconscious disappointment that looms with them and they wonder what might have been. When they consciously think about engaging their dreams, the black cloud of despair, disappointment and regret hits them and they will never endeavor in it because they are afraid of failing – after all, everyone told them they would fail!

So many people fear success and embrace failure. The right thing to do would be to embrace success but instead they hold onto and ruminate in their failure. Most people find satisfaction in life because they are doing the thing they believe is the right thing to do. Furthermore, they are doing the right thing because it is the right thing to do! Make sense? Remember, you are a spiritual being and inside you if you listen closely you will find all of the guidance that you need. It was over the years of listening to what everyone else was telling that you turned your filter off and let that seep in and deter from what your spirit was leading you to do. Also, many of those telling you what you should do and could be came from those who were not having their own esteem needs met and will never become self-actualized. If you will, it was the misguided leading the misguided. Sheesh!

When you surrender your dreams to fear and failure you are not doing the right thing! In fact, you are being selfish to others, yourself and of course God or the Higher Power who put the potentiality for great success in your mind and heart – your spirit. So after a while people surrender to righteous (living to their true potential) for three reasons:

1) They are afraid of failing. It is easier to risk nothing and remain status quo, than step out onto the ledge and bring exceedingly, abundant success. Check out the victor's motto. What do you think?

T**HE VICTOR'S MOTTO: I WOULD RATHER ATTEMPT TO DO SOMETHING GREAT AND FAIL TRYING, THAN ATTEMPT TO DO NOTHING AND SUCCEED AT NOTHING!**

Now check out the individual who is fearful and remains in the status quo or less. What do you think of this motto?

T**HE STATUS QUO MOTTO: I WOULD RATHER ATTEMPT TO DO NOTHING AND HOLD ONTO WHAT I HAVE AND NOT LOSE IT...WHO KNOWS WHAT THE FUTURE HOLDS?**

Which one do you prefer? Which one do you believe has and holds the secret to living a truly abundant life? Fear creates and perpetuates irrational thoughts and beliefs which hold people back. After fear immobilizes them, regret and depression set in and they look for ways to mask it, distract it, or completely numb it (substance use and abuse).

2) A second reason people choose not to live righteously is they are inclined to believe they are not ready to do so. Some people believe it (living righteously and successfully) will magically show up in their lives when they are worthy and deserving of it. Good luck with that one! Furthermore, if and when this magical event does show up in their lives, they then believe it wasn't meant for them, they are still not worthy of it, or they have to hold onto this knowledge and some day grow into it.

Some people are just downright lazy in their thinking and habits. This is also their excuse for being a cop-out. They believe if they are not worthy or ready to live successful and righteous lives, then they have the excuse they need to engage in the same detrimental lifestyles such as: alcoholism, drugs, pornography, gambling, sexual abuse, lying, cheating, etc. Even though many know they are on a collision course with self-destruction, many are taught to believe they have to "bottom out" and pay for their sins before they can be made right and worthy to walk the path of righteousness.

3) Some individuals just do not know any better...really! They may have been raised in abusive, dysfunctional and/or addictive familial environments. This is what they have engrained in their minds even though their spirits tell them there is something more. They close off that spiritual nagging because they possess low self-esteem, feel uncomfortable doing anything outside of their norm of existence to that point, and they fear they will let others down, even God/the Universal Mind!

I hear people all the time say things like, "This is the way things have always been and always will be... Who am I to try anything different?" I have even heard these people rationalize they do not want to do anything differently as they don't want to do better than their parents/grandparents and show them up. They believe that by doing better, they would be insulting their parents! So they choose to follow the footsteps of their parents and their parents' parents, etc. and you see this pattern of addiction and abuse continue from one generation to the next. If they would only try something that would bring them success and righteousness, this generational pattern could be broken for good!

How does one get to the point of truly doing what is right? I believe it is all about forgiveness, self-respect, and respecting others. It's not about appeasing and pleasing others, rather than acting on the righteous urges of what is within the soul. You can appease and please others but is it the right thing to do in all circumstances? Are they the right people you want to please and honor? How many times did you do something to appease someone only to feel bad inside after because you know you compromised your values, judgments and beliefs? Conversely, how did you feel when you know you did the right thing (that which in your soul told you it was right) but it went against what someone else wanted?

When you develop and feed your esteem needs you are on the right path to becoming self-actualized. In order to do this, you learn that you do the right thing because it is the right thing to do even when others treat you badly or judge you. Compromising yourself compromises your soul – you go against your essence. When you do this, there is a feeling of unrighteousness in you and you are always looking for ways to hide it, mask it or distract it. Bad habits and addictions are usually the answer because you try to feed from the outside what is eating away at you on the inside!

EXERCISE FOUR

In this exercise you are going to learn what it is to be human, who cares if you make a mistake and that it is never too late to just do it – what you want most! You are going to plant new seeds to build and increase self-esteem.

PART ONE

What are you most afraid of or failing at? I want you to make a list and write in depth what you are afraid of. I then want you to examine these fears and analyze them. You are to play detective and see where they came from and when they started.

Fill out the following chart as follows:

I AM MOST AFRAID OF FAILING AT OR FEAR MOST...	AS BEST AS I CAN REMEMBER IT STARTED WHEN...

Now I want you to refute and dispute the irrational belief surrounding the fears. After all that is what they are! They happened in the past and have no bearing on now...really! Really, get over it! I know this sounds gruff and it is meant to. I want you thinking this way and letting go of the past and accepting that you are no longer a prisoner to it. You paid your dues by holding onto these, even when you weren't required to. So, now is the time to let them all go. LET THEM GO!

Now I want you to complete the following chart the same way. Notice the slant has now changed in your favour. You are no longer afraid; rather, you are in total control of the present:

I AM NOT AFRAID NOR FEAR DOING...	BECAUSE OF THIS, I CAN NOW ACCOMPLISH AND I FEEL...

Great, you nailed it! Now I want you to focus on readiness.

PART TWO

How ready are you to be the person you were intended to be and want to be? Let's get to it! I want you to fill out the following chart being as honest as possible with yourself, focusing on the current moment:

What area(s) in your life right now do you believe need changing and why?	Why can't you make this change now? What are you waiting for to make it "feel right"?

Righteous living will only come when you feel worthy and deserving. Guess what? You are already worthy and deserving.

For those who want to create mantras/daily inspirations I would suggest saying something such as:

I am ready for positive change and success and embrace it with open arms. It is a personal right to be happy and feel good and I consciously feed both my conscious and unconscious positive thoughts that inspire me to feel good about myself and succeed at what I want most!

I have found this works great! People who have used this method have found great results. The reason it works is because it all starts with a simple belief in yourself. If you do not believe in yourself over the long haul who will? After a while, those who did will stop when they realise that you don't share the same belief in you!

PART THREE

Whatever in your life you feel deficient in, change it! If you lack self-esteem get individual counselling and/or join a support group. I also strongly advise signing up for short courses on self-esteem building. There are great books and meditation tapes on the subject. Google self-esteem resources on the Internet and you will be pleasantly surprised what you will find. There is something for everyone at whatever point they are in their lives.

Always remember even though you may have been raised by dysfunctional parents or in dysfunctional families, that is not you! You are ready to move on and reclaim your self-esteem. You know what you are afraid of, see it as irrational and have made it a non-issue. You are ready now as you are whole inside and have the right to feel and be righteous. So now, you just have to hold onto your self-esteem. Practise using positive quotes daily committing them to memory. These will serve as your personal self-esteem boosters and they work! Whenever you have a negative thought creep in, repeat your self-esteem boosters. You must practice them for at least 28 days and then you will feel and be better as they will be a permanent part of your mind. Once and for all, you will feel and be "right with yourself"!

CHAPTER NINE:

FORGIVENESS – HEALS THE MIND, BODY AND SOUL!

"Forgiveness means letting go of the past."

Gerald Jampolsy

"What goes around comes around!"
"Karma will find you!"
"What you give is what you get!"

Do any of these sound familiar to you?

Often times these are based on fear, threats or trying to get even. How many times did you say any of these statements with the hope of creating fear by foreshadowing in evening up a score? We all have free will and choice. This is based on attitude and intention. All attitude and intention holds power. How are you using the power of your attitude?

First comes CHOICE whenever a wrong doing is done to you. You have two options, basically, which are either to forgive and/or forget and move on, or you can harbour anger, resentment based on non-forgiveness in your mind, heart and soul. Obviously the former allows you to move on and enjoy your everyday living. The latter, holding onto things causes you to become embittered and resistant to peace of mind. This will only cause you misery and remember what misery loves? The company of more misery! This CHOICE you have either to "move on" or hold on" is based on ATTITUDE. What is your attitude about what happened to you going to be?

They say enjoying your everyday life is contingent most on attitude. It's not really about what happens to you, rather more about the attitude you have in how you choose to respond. A bitter heart, mind, and spirit will choose to respond bitterly. A happy heart, mind and spirit will respond by accepting what happened but taking something positively from the experience and choosing to move on. Which side of the teeter-totter are you on? If you are on the bitterness side, then you are probably feeling weighted down. On the other hand if you are on the acceptance side, there is a bounce in your step no doubt and you are feeling buoyant!

Attitude is all about reaction. It shouldn't be so much about what happens to you, rather how you choose to respond. How did you choose to react when something not so good (bad) happened to you? Some people become so filled with getting even or exacting revenge that this becomes their distorted sense of fulfillment. When you feel this way it is impossible for you to feel any sort of joy in your life. Your mind is focussed on thoughts that are filled with spite and evening up the score. This does nothing more than become solidified bitterness. The more you feed into it the more it continues to grow and eventually becomes petrified in your unconscious as a part of you. Not good!

When you operate from this mindset – getting even, then you are not being merciful, rather spiteful. Really! What kind of response do you actually think you are going to receive from those who you are spiteful and bitter toward? Do you think through some magical osmosis process that those you are being hurtful toward are going to offer you up the reverse and give you love, kindness, joy and peace? Probably not! When you come out bitter and swinging, people will usually mirror what you are projecting upon them. Even when they do give in and offer some better feeling than what you have given them, they will always be on guard around you. In the end, your attitude is better served when it is one of mercy, forgiveness and loving that person, or forgiving the situation.

In essence, whatever you send out will always come back to you. Some times what comes back to you is magnified, weight with much more than what you originally sent out. Bottom line: be careful for not only what you wish for, but also for what you send out as well! If you've ever been hit by a returning boomerang with greater momentum you will know it doesn't feel too good!

No one can be happy and miserable at the same time. It is impossible to harness two completely opposite, conflicting emotions. You cannot sow seeds based on hatred, loathing and resentment and grow situations of peace, joy, love and happiness. In order to change your world, you have to first start by changing yourself which is basically the beliefs and attitudes that you hold onto. Mahatma Gandhi put it best when he said, "You must be the change you want to see in the world." If you want to see mercy showed unto you, you must first demonstrate it in your own life. You can try your best to change your outer world (people and situations outside of you) but your inner world (you and your self-concept based on attitudes and beliefs) remains the same. You are the common denominator in your world.

Truly, no one can truly hurt your feelings unless you let them. Only you can allow yourself to be easily offended. They keep to being merciful is learning not to be so easily offended! No one can control you or your emotions unless you give them control. If you are giving them control, what does that say about you? Perhaps you are afraid you think and feel for yourself that you want someone else to do that for you? Maybe you have been in a co-dependent relationship for so long that you forgot what it is really like to think and feel your own feelings. Either way, when you blame someone else for "making you feel" a certain way you are really copping out! You are giving others credit they do not deserve.

Gandhi had another wonderful quote, "An eye for an eye only ends up making the whole world blind!" How true! So many people go through life thinking about how to get even, rather than learning how to truly forgive and move on. When you choose not to forgive, you truly pass on the belief that another person's past actions control you, which of course, we know isn't true at all. At some unconscious level, though, you do attribute power and control over yourself to another's actions. It's funny how the mind can trick you into believing and buying into these silly irrational patterns.

In order to be merciful and do merciful things, people need to not only look for the good in others, but believe there is goodness in everyone. When you empathize and even help another individual with their concerns, it helps you become a better person. It also takes your mind off your own worries and concerns. Being of service to others helps you to become more empathetic, understanding and patient around others. This is a simple formula for not only true happiness in your life but also what allows "mercy" and forgiveness to be a staple attitude in your life. As Gandhi put it, "Man (woman) becomes great exactly in the degree in which he works for the welfare of his fellow-men."

Remember, when you give a little, you get a little back. When you give a lot you get a lot back. The key is to simply give! In this case the key is to not only show forgiveness to others but also yourself which begins with forgiving yourself for your thoughts, feelings and actions. When you are able to do this then you will truly release the thoughts that bind you to bitter resistance. Those are the deepest wounds and hurts that people carry around with them, sometimes their entire lives. When you have wounds that continually gush with hurt and shame, you try your best to shut them off and when you can't, then you try to mask them. Alcohol, drugs and other addictions and bad habits are big time reminders that something that requires forgiveness resides below the surface of your mind. Once you are ready to show others and yourself mercy, you are ready to finally release this two-headed ugly monster of bitter resistance.

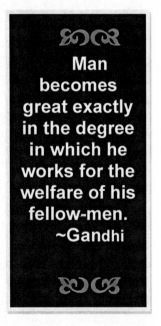

Man becomes great exactly in the degree in which he works for the welfare of his fellow-men. ~Gandhi

Perhaps the most amusing, sarcastic, even absurd thing about not forgiving others or showing them mercy is often times they do not even know you are upset with them. They have moved on, shrugged off what happened, or even forgiven you. And here you are holding onto the poison, taking bitter sips of it, waiting for someone else to come and take it from you. You need to let go! Forgiveness is the sweetest drink you will ever allow to pass your lips!

EXERCISE FIVE

IDENTIFYING AND BEING FORGIVENESS

If you want forgiveness to show up in your life then you have to forgive others. When you want to be forgiven you must first know how to forgive. It is the same for love – in order to truly be loved, you must first learn to love yourself in order to give love to others.

I want you to work through the following chart and fill it out as in much detail as possible:

I HAVE NOT FORGIVEN THIS ASPECT OF MYSELF – SOMETHING I HAVE OR HAVE NOT DONE FOR ME...	WHEN DID THIS EVENT OCCUR AND WHY DO I BELIEVE I HAVE HELD ONTO NOT FORGIVING ME?	IN FORGIVING MYSELF FOR THIS, WHAT WOULD IT DO FOR ME AND HOW WOULD IT HELP ME?

The last part of this non-forgiveness chart which focuses on the lack of forgiveness you have for yourself helps you to identify grudges that you hold against yourself. These grudges that you hold against you get transferred on to others and you then have difficulties forgiving them. The third column "IN FORGIVING MYSELF FOR THIS, WHAT WOULD IT DO FOR ME AND HOW WOULD IT HELP ME?" is the most important as you are now able to recognize and see what your lack of forgiveness toward yourself is doing to you and by overcoming it, how much better your attitude will become.

In this next chart, I want you to do much the same as you did in the first chart, but this time you are going to look at how your attitude toward non-forgiveness is transferred onto others:

I HAVE NOT FORGIVEN SOMEONE FOR WHAT THEY DID TO ME. THEY DID THIS...	WHEN DID THIS EVENT OCCUR, WHY DO I BELIEVE I HAVE HELD ONTO NOT FORGIVING THEM AND WHAT'S IN IT FOR ME?	IN FORGIVING OTHERS FOR WHAT THEY HAVE DONE, IT WOULD FINALLY HELP ME FEEL/BE?

Like the first chart, the completion of this one helps you develop feelings of liberation and self-efficacy. You get to be the one on control and be free from the past! In the third column, you are identifying what forgiving others will do for you, rather than what you have carried in your mind, "What it will do for them!" Sure forgiving someone is great for that person, they feel accepted, but forgiving them for your own sense of peace is even better. You stop drinking the poison and waiting for them to keel over! You have set yourself free. Too many people who choose to drink the proverbial "poison" are left with bitter tastes in their mouths. Hemlock is rarely served in restaurants! Instead, people try to wash away the taste with booze or drugs. Guess what? The horrible taste becomes imprinted on your taste buds until you forgive and set it free as well as others.

Your mercy is the only thing that can return your emotional taste buds to their natural state.

CHAPTER TEN:

HAVING FAITH IN YOURSELF AND YOUR ABILITIES!

"A faith is a necessity to man. Woe to him who believes in nothing."

Victor Hugo

Some people are afraid to better themselves because they feel they might experience failure even worse. "I am already a failure and I live my life less than half pure, I can only imagine the anxiety it would cause me to try and live better only to fail!" some would say. They believe this would set them up for greater failure and only make them feel worse. If they weren't engaging in bad habits, or drinking and drugging to mask their shame of failure now, imagine what it would be like after trying to act better only to fail harder? The goal in achieving spiritual growth is achieving faith in oneself!

Humans were designed with built-in "faith" mechanisms. Humans possess an amazing quality in their spirits – faith. This faith is the personality characteristic which helps people transcend to the highest levels of their imagination and being. It is the ultimate quality you will possess within your self-esteem, which will bring you to that place you yearn to achieve – self-actualization. In order to get there, you have to possess "mountain moving faith" or at least enough to start out with to move the tiniest of mole hills and building up to moving foothills, and then the mountains you dream of moving.

Building faith is like building muscles. You have to exercise it and allow it to grow over time with repeated use and practice. This all begins with being you best self and trying your best!

In order to overcome all doubts and fears in your life you have to have faith. In essence, to enjoy truly great everyday living you have to live by faith.

Faith is something that is innate in human beings. True faith is expecting the positive to happen. Too many people live with the cynical notion, "I hope for the best but expect the worst." What is that? The positive part in the state "best" gets negated by the negative part "worst". Furthermore, the word "expect" is more absolute, definitive and powerful than the word "hope". Guess what? When you live according to that motto, you are setting up situations for yourself that will usually land on the side of "worst". After all, that is what you expected and you did put that order in to the Universe!

Our spirits are wired to have faith. Since we are created by a Divine and loving God who is the embodiment of faith, then we too should possess faith. Imagine if God/the Universal Mind was the ocean and we were but mere droplets of water from the ocean. If a chemist came along and tested our chemical make-up and compared it to the ocean, we would obviously possess the same make-up. Our overall concentration wouldn't be the same as the initial source, but we would have all the same attributes and qualities. So then if God/a Higher Power is the embodiment of spiritual faith, we too, then, must have all the abilities to possess this spiritual faith as well. We are humans housing the tremendous powers of spiritual faith!

If you are lacking in faith, how do you tap into it or develop it? Perhaps this is an equally challenging notion similar to believing that you must be pure. In this regard all it takes is simple belief! You have to believe in it in order for it to work. You are probably asking, "What or who must I believe in?" Great question. If you are a "believer" in the sense of God, then you should believe in not only God's promises, but also believe in yourself. If you do not believe in God or a Higher Power, then you, for sure, have to believe in yourself – in this case, you will never be anything positive without believing in yourself!

The first thing you need to do is remove any and all self-destructive thought patterns that you have that are leading to negative feelings. When you have negative thoughts creating depressing and bitter feelings, you are cutting yourself from the true essence of your spirit. You see, you are letting feelings/emotions rule you. Feelings are usually fleeting and all over the place. Since they are hard to harness and control, they are difficult to make sense of. Furthermore, when you do, you are usually too irrational to understand your thought process that is creating them.

The second thing that you need to do is remove yourself from anyone who is negative and lacks faith in them self. People who are lacking in faith can't help you build your own faith. They are incapable of adding anything to your life or accenting you in a positive way. The more you associate with negative and self-destructive people, the more likely you are to become just like them. Avoid them!

When people endure repeated frustrations, disappointment and hurts which lead to anxiety and depression, they create a tunnel vision process based on anxiety and frustration. Negative emotions will cause you to become blinded to the positive thoughts/feelings that exist. Furthermore, negative emotions will make you "negative" and will sever your connection to God, the Higher Power where the root of your faith exists.

Have you ever heard the expression, "I need to see it to believe it?" Well, that is the cynic's point of view. The individual who possesses faith thinks more along the lines of, "When I believe it, then I will see it!" Too many people operate on the premise of, "Seeing is believing," and look where that is getting them. It's all about lining your faith up with God/a Higher Power, or that innate spiritual part of you. When you develop psychological and spiritual health you are on the right track to "spiritual purity" – TRUE FAITH!

Avoid making and basing major decisions on doubts and pessimisms. When you do you are letting feelings seep in to play. These feelings are usually negative in origin and usually are rooted in fear, guilt, rejection, failure, and/or anxiety. These emotions are "faith blockers". They render you feeling helpless and usually cause you to withdraw. When this happens, you are less likely to move ahead and create positive change for yourself. Also, you are more likely to wallow in your sorrow which might mean drinking, drugging or compulsive eating, etc. to try to drown it out. This only further separates you from the faith you have deep within yourself (personal belief in you) as well as God/the Universal Mind. Whatever is interfering with your ability to find faith in yourself and/or God/the Universal Mind you need to find. Only after you find the resentments, hurts, and even the hateful mindset will you be able to connect with spiritual faith. When you do, you will find God/a Higher Power and definitely SWEET ACCEPTANCE for your entire spiritual being. You actually find "YOU"! So many people go through life asking the question, "Who am I?" Instead, they should be asking, "Why did I block myself off from my spiritual self, and where can I find ME?" Seek and you will find!

Ask and it will be given to you; seek and you will find; knock and the door will be opened to you.
~ **Matthew 7:7**

Too many people are too proud to ask and would rather run in place on a treadmill hoping to go somewhere. Too many people live their lives with blinders on either because they are afraid of what they might see, especially within themselves. And too many are afraid to knock because they are afraid they will be rejected...even by themselves! Whatever is going to be in your life is totally up to you. Too many live with the notion, "Well, it wasn't meant to be!" Says who? Instead, you should be saying, "It is meant to be because it sure as heck is up to me!" Now doesn't that sound more empowering?

Asking is the first part of the process in succeeding at what you want. If you are a believer then ask God/a Higher Power for help, support and whatever it is you need. If you are not a believer then ask it of yourself. Remember, inside you is spirit/soul and that it your innateness. Your mind will help you connect with the right sources and situations for you to achieve your desire.

Believing is the second part. You need to believe in God/a Higher Power or yourself to know that what you want is possible, doable and attainable. Believing means going forth as if your request has not only been a possibility, but will become a fact.

Finally, you need to receive. Act and pretend that what you want or who you want to be is a reality. Remember, throughout this book, I have asserted that if you think it, you will start to feel it, and then you will act accordingly and eventually become it. If your life is dysfunctional or in ruins, the proof is already in the pudding as you are following this energy flow in a negative way. Now, it is time to engage it in a positive way. Interestingly, when you start to focus on the positive, you will attract more positive into your life. You see, the law of attraction is always at work. The key is to shift into a positive mindset to get the proverbial ball rolling. Please refer to the following chart to learn more about how this process to receiving (intention on the positive) works:

ASK
- I ask God, the Divine, a Higher Power or the Universe for what I want most
- I ask myself to fulfill or become the desire I seek

BELIEVE
- Know that what you want/desire is possible as all things are possible with God!
- Know that within you have the tools, means and energies to create or transform yourself or situation into what you want.

RECEIVE
- Have faith in God /a Higher Power that what you asked for and believe in is a reality even though you don't see it. It takes time and the time will be right to suit your needs.
- Act as if you are the person you've asked to become or have the situation you desire most as you will attract it based on the energy you are creating for yourself and projecting outward.

RECEIVING FORMULA

155

As you can see from the chart I describe the ASK, BELIEVE and RECEIVE flow of energy which is faith-based from both a spiritual perspective and cognitive perspective. Those who are able to incorporate "faith building" both ways will see tremendous results in time!

Faith starts out with belief. Even if it is the tiniest belief it is still a belief and enough to get you started. Getting started is the key! When you move into the following exercise, imagine that all things are possible and do not be afraid to ask of God/a Higher Power as well yourself.

EXERCISE SIX

PART ONE

I want you to write out situations from your past where you wanted something so bad and were disappointed that it didn't happen the way you wanted it to, or you did not get what you wanted. Write out the feelings in detail to each of these disappointments. Really get into the feeling. Now I want you to release these feelings as being nothing more as frozen in time in the past contingent upon that "disappointing situation" and they have no bearing on your here and now, or your future. Negative feelings are okay to have as they are part of being human. Holding onto them is not okay because you were meant to live a happy, joyful life.

I want you to become a photographer during this exercise. With eyes closed I want you to recall the disappointing experience and the feeling. I want you to flip a switch in your mind where you frame this experience just as you would a picture. Once framed in your mind, imagine changing its colour to black and white. Make it look like an old fashioned photo from the past. When you turn something to black and white, as well as perceive it from being in the past it loses much of whatever energy or power it possesses. Keep doing this until you see these frame pictures in black and white. When you have achieved this, I want you to put those photos in an old storage trunk in your mind and lock it away. If you have a wonderfully vivid imagination, see yourself standing on the deck of a boat sailing at sea. The chest rests at the edge of the ship and one little push will send it over to the greatest depths where you will never see it or find it ever again. Go for it – push it over!

PART TWO

In this exercise you are going to complete your own ASK, BELIEVE AND RECEIVE energy flowchart. You can and will use this exercise to change any area of your life that you feel needs changing, or you can use it to add/request things you want of yourself and/or God/the Universal Mind. Really have fun with this, remembering the sky is the limit!

Make copies of this to use this process ongoing. It really does work!

ASKING

I ask God/a Higher power to help me attain _____ for my life. I know my life will be better and improve if I have _____.

I ask of myself /inner spirit to bring me _____ in my life as I know the quality of my life will improve if I have _____.

BELIEVING

I am believing God/Higher Power for _____ this to happen in my life right now!

I am believing in myself/inner spirit to bring me _____!

RECEIVING

Having attained _____ makes me feel _____. This feeling for having _____ right now is so exhilerating. (Get into the feeling of having!) I am so thankful to God/a Higher Power!

Having attained _____ makes me feel so _____. This feeling of _____ only adds to confidence in my personal abiltiies and control over my life! (Embrace the feeling!)

This exercise helps **SWEET ACCEPTANCE** to grow and flourish.

CHAPTER ELEVEN:

RESPECTING AND MAKING PEACE WITH YOURSELF!

"Am I not destroying my enemies when I make friends of them?"

Abraham Lincoln

In this chapter the essence is about caring – caring for others because we care about ourselves. People do the right thing because they care about doing the right thing! Whenever you choose to do the right thing, you do so out of a sense of honour, integrity and personal dignity. These three components create what we have discussed in previous chapters as well as throughout this book – self-esteem. You manufacture a great sense of self-esteem in doing the right thing and keeping peace. Furthermore, this increases your sense of self-worth as well allowing you to stand dignified which equates with a sense of increased self-respect. Always remember, no one is going to give you the respect you deserve and want to feel unless you first learn to respect yourself!

Too many people try to be something they are not. They get caught up in being pleasers or skipping to the beat of another person's drum. Some get caught up in abusive situations and feel trapped and eventually get trapped. Many people do not know any better as this is how they were raised and generational abuse has always continued to flourish. And some make really bad choices to just fit in – to be one of the crowd! How many people started their smoking, drinking or drugging as a teenager because the "in-crowd" was doing it? They wanted to feel and be cool. They wanted to be accepted. Interestingly, they may or may not have felt accepted by the crowd they were trying to please, but when they became addicted or developed extremely bad habits, they try their best to hide doing it because they worry if others find out, they won't be accepted. What a contradiction! As a teen/young adult they used to feel/get accepted (it was cool to feel out of control) and as an adult, you do your best not to use/abuse substances because that will get you kicked out of positive social norms (as you appear out of control). In the end, it is all about keeping the peace – within yourself! Without inner self-peace, you feel like your life is crumbling, going to shambles and any peace you ever had seems like it is going to pieces!

You can't move forward trying to teach peace unless you first know how it feels, and only then will you be able to offer it. Too many people believe that they have to use aggression, even violence to create peace. And that includes peace within themselves. Using and abusing alcohol, drugs or whatever harmful vice is self-inflicted harm/violence. You are only hurting yourself.

In order to promote peace on the inside and out for yourself, you have to remove the inner conflict that rages inside you. You need to make peace with yourself. You have to learn that it is much easier to paddle downstream with the current than it is to try and paddle against the current. Too many people are quick to jump the gun and get into conflict and arguments with others before weighing out options for responding. Too many people react out knee-jerk responses. This has become habitually engrained in them as they have learned to respond this way for way too long! In fact, the conflictual/inner dialogue is already going on inside them before they have even weighed all of the facts, or while they haven't even allowed the other person to finish their sentence. They revert to their conditioned, negative old way of responding. They come out swinging! Does this sound familiar to you?

It is only after they have weighed out in their minds what they did or said was wrong that their consciences kick in and they feel really bad. How many people drink or drug, or engage in some bad habit for hours, days, weeks all because of one 5 minute disagreement or argument that shouldn't have even gotten to that point in the first place? It's funny how something that shouldn't have even become something big or "blown out of proportion" can cause someone to "slip", "lapse", "relapse", "fall off of the wagon", or continue to engage in addictive behaviors as they don't have all of the facts, or the facts are irrationally misconstrued. The key to creating and maintaining a mind of peace is to follow a simple three-step process:

1) Get the facts straight!

Let the other person finish speaking before interrupting or responding. Too many people jump to conclusions based on past experiences. They respond by default. In essence, they respond without thinking. This also applies to you! Get the facts straight within your own mind. Develop an active mindset, rather than a passive one using facts from previous situations to make judgments on the current matter at hand. You see, when you use past judgments, you are more likely to respond in the present as you have done so in the past. You are like a mechanical robot reacting on an outdated computer programme rather than recreating new programmes as you go along.

2) Think before responding!

Too many people fly off the handle or are in a hurry to say or do something. I believe this is often the result of "instant gratification" and entitlement. They believe if they don't strike while the "iron is still" hot, their message/action will lose its effectiveness. When you think things out you demonstrate to others as well as yourself you are in control. Remember, you are mighty (calm) because you can control your thoughts and emotions. Guess what? This makes you a "mastermind" in that you are the master of your mind!

3) Choose a response that will try to make things better!

To be a peace-maker is to respond in a way that creates less harm and strives toward a positive resolution. When you fly off the handle you are not making things better! Furthermore, when you drink to drown your sorrows, drug to mask the anger/hurt, or compulsively eat to punish your shame, you are not making matters better. Brainstorm the best possible response(s) before responding or simply walk away to collect your thoughts so you are able to keep the peace – most notably the peace within yourself!

I know this is simple communication 101, but too many people take the simple for granted and get caught up in doing things in a ridiculous, irrational complex manner! The key is to practice responding this way in order to succeed at being the peaceful person you were designed to be.

I am going to suggest some excellent methods for "peace-keeping". These methods are great for working with others, as well as the inner conflicts within your own mind. I use those often in working with individuals with addictions, anger management training as well as self-esteem building. Read through these 3 methods as you will have a chance to use them in Exercise Seven.

PERSPECTIVE TAKING

This approach is very much like assertiveness training. In assertiveness training, one of the key elements is reflective listening. Most reflective listening training and skills come from the wonderful work of Carl Rogers and his Client-centered Therapy approach. I strongly recommend reading some of his books to master these skills.

Reflective listening skills are at the heart of perspective taking and can often de-escalate conflict and confrontations before they get out of hand. The two major ingredients for reflective listening are:

1) Listening with intention/active listening
2) Paraphrasing

Listening with intention requires listeners to become active participants in the conversation, not only in speaking but also in listening. When most people communicate, they think of what they are going to say or how they will answer while the other person is talking. Rather than fully devoting their undivided attention to the speaker, they are contemplating possible responses.

Listening with intention involves just what it implies. You listen to both the denotation and connotation of the speech. Denotation is the superficial surface level dialogue others offer us when they speak. Denotation is the simple spoken word. The gist of what is said. Connotation on the other hand is the emotional, subjective meaning underlying the words. Connotation provides the ingredients which gives words true meaning. Always remember, words don't mean, people do!

To listen with intention means listening for the true meaning within spoken words. Rather than analyzing the words themselves, active listening requires the listener to seek out the true intention for what was said. When you focus on the intention of words spoken, your mind no longer has time to dwell on confrontational and aggressive responses. If you are a hothead always waiting for the chance to respond to further fuel the argument, this approach might save headache and regret.

Sometimes people say things they don't mean or say things in the heat of the moment without thinking first. Their subjectivity over-rides their objectivity. Many prolonged arguments and fall-outs are the result of misspoken or unintended words. You are in control of your mind and body. How you decide to respond is up to you. Remember, no one can make you angry! That decision is totally up to you. My guess is, if you have a personality which thrives on conflict and manipulation, then you are probably chomping at the bit to fire counter-attacks during arguments. In fact, you are most likely an individual who likes to strike below the belt or launch stored up grievances at the other person. When you are too busy listening with intention, you are distracting yourself from your own irrational thought process, your need to argue.

What would you think if I said, *"It's raining cats and dogs"*? If you listen without intention, then you are just listening to the spoken words. You probably say to yourself, *"so what, big deal!"*

On the other hand, when you listen with intention to, *"it's raining cats and dogs"*, you might see I have offered you something a little more profound than just the basic spoken words. I might have actually uttered this statement because I care about you, it's cold and rainy, and I don't want you to catch a cold. Argumentative people usually pay attention to the superficial part of this statement and get ready to say something sarcastic in return. *"What do you think, I am an idiot and blind that I can't see that it is raining?"* You may even take the implication the other person is insulting you and asserting you are incapable of taking care of yourself. On the other hand, the subjective meaning implies the other person really cares about you and your well-being. Funny, sometimes we disagree over something we are in total agreement over due to the interpretation and intention of the remarks people make.

Paraphrasing is the process of seeking clarification or reaffirming what the other person has said. Paraphrasing is putting into your own words what the other person has said to you. It clarifies to you and the speaker the true intention and meaning for what has been said. This alone can prevent misunderstandings and ugly arguments. Clarification is important as it guards against making assumptions.

The major goal of perspective taking is to keep the lines of communication open. If you possess aggression, practising this approach shows others you are open-minded and willing to listen. If you were to continue to practise your rigid thinking process and be less responsive to listening to others, you will soon get the label *"stubborn"* or *"hardhead"*. People will not want to talk to you because they know all you want to do is argue. They will perceive you as not wanting to listen to them because what they have to say is less important. I cannot reiterate this point enough! Perspective taking gets you out of your combative attitude as it obstructs your argumentativeness and encourages listening. If you want to see the quality of your relationships and social interactions improve, I strongly recommend using this approach!

OWN YOUR FEELINGS!

Whenever I work with clients one on one, or in anger management groups, one of the first points I present to them is that no one person can make you angry unless you allow yourself to become angry. Not surprisingly, clients strongly object to my *"ridiculous'* statement. I usually smile at them and ask them if they think I could make them do something against their will. I've even gone so far as to ask, *"Could I be your God or, better yet, some perverse puppeteer who can make you do whatever I want, even making you angry?'* Of course they think about it for a moment. Before they are ready to offer me an answer, I badger them with another quick question, *"Do you think your wife, husband, boss, or* whoever *makes you mad is God of your life?"* They usually offer me a very definitive *"No!"* I then have them stop in their tracks and ask them to rethink what they were just trying to convince me of. Here is the line of reasoning I provide them with:

"Okay, it is your spouse, or boss who makes you angry, right? Well, if they can make you angry, then I am sure they are responsible for all of your other emotions as well, joy, sadness, fear, etc. Right? Just think about what you are telling me! Furthermore, think about what you are trying to convince yourself of. You are leading yourself to believe others are responsible for what you are feeling or not feeling. You are basically an empty emotional mind waiting to be fed and filled by others. Also, once filled, you become a puppet. They can then make you dance around however way they choose. You are pretty much like a monkey dancing around to the sounds of the organ the puppeteer is grinding. Poor you! Sounds like you can't make any emotional decisions for yourself. They truly are God to you. How does that make you feel?"

At this point, there is usually a prolonged moment of silence as my clients ponder what I have just said. The silence is usually broken by a nervous laugh, snorting, head-shaking or knee slapping. The response I hear next is one I'd swear was memorized by each client, *"Wow, I never thought of it that way!"* Once more, there is usually a prolonged silence as my clients ponder this new revelation. Almost like clockwork the next comment or question they make is always the same, *"It's only my wife who gets under my skin." "It's only my husband who annoys the heck out of me!" "My kids are on my last nerve." "I hate my boss and my place of work!"*

I want you to remember the following:

1) You own your feelings and only you can feel your emotions.
2) No one can control you unless you let them.
3) Even when you let someone control you, you are still in total control as you choose how you will allow them to manipulate you.
4) Accusing others for making you mad or creating other emotions in you allows you to try to escape responsibility for what you are thinking and feeling.
5) No one including yourself can make you feel angry unless you first think something to stimulate your emotions.
6) Only you can decide on whether to get angry or not.
7) The mind can only devote its full attention to one thing at a time! If someone around you is trying to engage you in a conflict and you are too busy meditating on God's word, the likelihood of you getting upset isn't very high!
8) Those you get angry with the most are usually people close to you who you have an emotional vested interest in.
9) Perhaps the reason you are really getting mad is you wish to be the puppeteer (controlling) and others are not co-operating with you!

10) Why should everything always have to go your way or be the way you like it? Perhaps you are a perfectionist putting too much pressure on yourself and others!

STAY IN THE PRESENT

Most people get a great sense of comfort from reliving emotions and experiences from the past. Interestingly, the emotions and experiences are not always pleasant ones! Some people prefer to hold onto negative experiences because it gives them a sense of perceived power or comfort.

Why do so many people choose to live in the past? The answer is quite simple. They derive a sense of comfort from the past because it is non-threatening. They already know what has happened. The future has yet to come so they have no control over the future. The same can be said about the past. We have no control over the past because it has already happened. We cannot go back and change it!

The only time frame we possess total control over is the present. What I find most interesting when I work with clients is they resist feeling and existing in the present the most! The reason why is that they have to invest thought and emotion in the present and for some, this is quite threatening! Furthermore, to work in the present means to change existing negative thought patterns. This takes a lot of work and some people are not willing to invest the time, energy or emotions. They hold onto what they know, even though it is detrimental and negative, rather than risk gaining something more positive. Generally speaking, when it comes to self-analysis and change, most people are lazy!

If time traveling machines in movies really existed, then life truly would be so much easier. You could go back and change things. Unfortunately, these movies are fantastical. Your negative/irrational thought patterns are real and require change!

In essence, you have to create your own mental time traveling machine which will keep your emotions in the present state. This is paramount when you are involved with people you perceive as having wronged you in the past. I am sure you are able to transport yourself back in time in a blink of an eye to the unfortunate situation you were a part of involving the other person. This gets the juices flowing, the pulse racing and the angry/negative thoughts recurring all over again. You need to stop this if you are ever going to move on!

There are several questions I ask clients to think about when discussing their anger/negative thinking:

1) How is getting angry/upset today undoing what happened in the past?
2) How is getting angry/upset now making you feel good in the present?
3) Can you actually go back and change what happened?
4) Do you think those who did wrong to you still dwell on what happened and get as upset as you?
5) Do you believe you are in control of yourself right here, right now in the present?
6) If you answered yes to the last question, what do you want to feel right now? What would make you feel great?
7) If vengeance or ill harm is wished upon the person from the past, then you are not living in the present! How can you get into a positive, present feeling state now? What is a positive, happy thought for you now?
8) What goals would you like to set for yourself which will make you a *"present"* thinker?

I like to spend at least one session going through this process to allow clients to recognize a few things:

1) You can only control the present.
2) Only you control your thoughts, feelings and actions.
3) The past will always remain unchanged.

4) Your present will soon become the past and wouldn't you rather build on healthier pasts?
5) Anything you choose to be or do is up to you.

If you want to have a life of peace and self-respect, you must first seek and become the respect you want to share!

EXERCISE SEVEN

PART ONE – PERSPECTIVE TAKING

I would like you to recall the most recent disagreement you had with another person. I want you to evaluate it. Do you really know what they were telling you or were you getting their intended message or were you too fixated on how you would respond? If you could go back and change anything about yourself while listening, what would it be?

Now the key here is to identify what it is you are telling yourself when listening to another person. You see, you shouldn't be telling yourself anything as you should be too busy listening. The problem with not listening to others is you don't get the right or intended message. Second, it shows your own perceptive/listening skills are lacking for your own inner dialogue. You are cluttering your mind with random thoughts, thoughts not related to or focused on the task at hand, or you are thinking about how you are going to answer your own thoughts without even letting yourself finish. Get my point?

ASSIGNMENT #1

I want you to perspective take on your own thinking. For the next little while, monitor your thoughts. Pay attention to your inner dialogue. Do you have a nagging voice that keeps interfering with you telling you negative things from the past? Does this negative voice act critical of another person when they are speaking to you? The goal here is to shoot down the negative thoughts and challenge them. Whenever you have this negative bantering going on your mind, respond one of the following ways to your inner thoughts by letting your inner voice correct the nagging voice;

"Not now, I am too busy listening to _____'s story!"

174

"The past is the past and has no bearing for what is going on current!"

"I appreciate that _____ is sharing with me and I choose to understand them as best as I can."

"Stop! I am too busy listening to..."

Use something like this to increase your empathetic listening skills, which will lead to better perspective taking.

If you are a believer in God/a Higher Power I want you to pay attention and listen to His voice which will be heard inside of you. The best way is to sit quietly, or meditate and wait for that voice to speak to you or inspire you. If you have a hard time with this, ask God a question and then sit quietly and await an answer.

PART TWO - OWN YOUR FEELINGS!

Perhaps the greatest inspiration is that God/a Higher Power gave us life and gave it to us in abundance. If this is true, then we are free. We can be whatever we want to be and no one owns us. We are free from thinking others control us. No one owns your feelings except you. Take back what God/the Universal Mind has given you...Free will to think and feel!

You are the master of your mind. You think the feelings you feel. Choose better thoughts that will give you better feelings!

ASSIGNMENT #2

For this assignment you are going to monitor your thoughts that provoke feelings. It is often times harder at first to monitor your thoughts, but easier to monitor your feelings because they are so intense. Bad feelings tell you that you are off kilter and need to refocus your thinking on a positive direction.

For the next 30 days, monitor your thoughts doing 2 things:

Whenever you get a negative thought, quickly identify it, name it and consciously say, "I don't like this thought as it is something I do not like feeling, so I actively choose this a better thought (peace, joy, happiness, love) which makes me feel good." Now focus on positive thoughts that provoke good feelings. If you have trouble with this, try remembering something or anything that makes you happy (a happy memory, someone you love, etc.) and focus on that for a moment and allow the positive feelings to flow from it. In doing so, you are creating a positive energy flow which will create more positive thoughts which produce more positive feelings.

Whenever you have positive feelings, really feed off them and feel the peace, joy and happiness they bring. Law of attraction asserts you will get more of what you focus on!

PART THREE – STAY IN THE PRESENT

The goal with this exercise is to focus all of your thoughts on the here and now.

You will learn autonomy, empowerment and hope by focusing on the present. Hourly, or moment to moment reminders help you to live in the present. Once you do this enough times, living in the present becomes second nature. In fact, you become so into living in the present it distracts your thought processes from drifting back into the past. You can't think of past wrongs done to you when you are thinking about feeling good right now!

ASSIGNMENT #3

For the next month, throughout the day remind yourself to stay in the present. Carry little cue cards, programme it on your laptop, cell phone or computer that focus on living in the present. Create nifty sayings like, "I choose to live in the present because the present is all I have right now!", or "The present is a gift from God/the Universal Mind...a perfect gift and that is all I currently need!" Come up with something that will help you stay grounded in the here and now. Trust me; this will work if you work this into your life for at least 28 days!

CHAPTER TWELVE:

LETTING GO OF THE PAST - ANGER, HURTS AND PAYBACKS

"The last of human freedoms - the ability to chose one's attitude in a given set of circumstances."

Viktor E. Frankl

This chapter truly embodies the concept of letting go! For those in spiritual programs, who have tried them, then the concept of "LET GO and LET GOD!" may resonate with you. When you constantly carry a chip on your shoulder because someone insulted you, hurt you or wronged you, then you will pretty much live a life of hell – negative, destructive thought patterns. Too many people get insulted too easily. They get offended and then grow hardened over it, trying to settle a score.

In life everyone will experience some kind of rejection, harassment, insult or discrimination. As long as you are human and have a heartbeat, no one is free from emotional hurts and putdowns. These experiences have the most profound effects on one's self-esteem. How you perceive these putdowns can make you stronger if you refuse to take them personally, or they have the ability to crush your self-esteem. Which side of the fence do you choose to stand on?

When people are "persecuted" that is, believing they have been wronged they can either try to even up the score or move on. Whether you are a believer in God/ a Higher Power or a believer in justice, you have to realize that vindication, vengeance and some sense of restorative justice will often times only come outside of your own means. Holding onto hurts and bitterness and wishing/hoping that those who hurt you will pay for their wrongs traps you in a place of victimization – fixated on the point of time when you were wronged and never moving on. Did you know this has the ability to stunt your emotional growth by keeping certain aspects of your emotional maturity linked to that event/situation? You need to let go and let God! If you don't subscribe to God/the Universal Mind, then let go and let life! Let your life happen and unfold day by day going forward rather than looking back in your rearview mirror focusing on what happened to you or what didn't happen. The key is moving forward and learning to say to yourself, "I will not be easily offended!"

Deep vengeance is the daughter of deep silence.
~ Vittorio Alfieri

There are also individuals who fight to avoid persecution in the form of rejection. Do you know of anyone or have you ever felt that you needed to do something that went against your beliefs in order to fit in with a particular group or crowd? If you didn't step up to the plate you worried what others would think about you. Before you knew it, you were using and/or addicted to cigarettes, alcohol, marijuana, pornography, gambling etc., because your friends were doing it, or those who you most wanted to fit in with were doing it. You didn't want to be ridiculed for not doing what "they" were doing. Ridicule would have meant being persecution!

Persecution based on righteousness is often based on perception. This perception derived from doing the right thing because inside it feels right. Furthermore, this feeling of being "right" comes from personal freedom – freedom to be and do whatever you want because you know it is right!

Viktor Frankl was the psychiatrist who was taken prisoner along with his family during World War II by the Nazis. As you know the Nazis under Hitler exterminated so many innocent people. Frankl watched his family and friends die around him, many of them because they had lost their will to live in the concentration camps. There was something that arose in Frankl that would later lead him to write one of the most amazing books of his time *Man's Search for Meaning*. The Nazis had taken everything away from Frankl: his family, his clothing, his freedom...his livelihood. Seeing his life crumbling around him, Frankl made a conscious effort to hold onto the one thing the Nazis could not take from him, his dignity. Frankl knew that his dignity was based on his own psychological freedom to think and feel. It was at that point he decided he would not allow them the satisfaction of crushing his human spirit – the connection to the spirit of his Higher Power. Frankl believed and eventually survived according to attitude, he thought it his way. To quote Frankl, "Everything can be taken from a man or a woman but one thing: the last of human freedoms to choose one's attitude in any given set of circumstances, to choose one's own way."

What have you given up in your life that has made you feel emotionally handicapped? Are you at a point in your life where you feel you have difficulty making the right choices because you waved your decision-making skills long ago succumbing to the whims, demands and threats of others? Do you find yourself addicted to drugs, alcohol, or engaged in bad, destructive habits because of choices you made in the past that wouldn't have been your first, second or even third choices? Do you believe your self-esteem has been compromised, even belittled over the years because of your bad choices – giving in to others? If you answered yes to any or all of these questions, then your time is now!

You see, to have the freedom you want in your life is all about attitude. It is not about what happens to you, rather how you respond to it.

> I am convinced that life is 10% what happens to me and 90% of how I react to it. And so it is with you... we are in charge of our attitudes.
>
> ~ **Charles R. Swindoll**

Your attitude in the here and now will be your greatest asset and friend, if you allow it in. A positive attitude will liberate you from your past misconceptions, irrational thinking and dysfunctional lifestyle. Throughout this book I have mentioned repeatedly that thoughts create feelings, not the other way around. By now you know you can change your feelings by changing your thoughts. It is all about changing your thinking – changing the attitudes that manufacture certain thinking patterns. Your time for an attitude adjustment is now! It is time to create solid attitudes that will create positive feelings that will produce good feelings.

Take a moment to study the following diagram. As you can see the positive flow of attitudinal energy will create good thoughts leading to positive feelings. Conversely, a negative flow of attitudinal energy will create bad thoughts which will lead you to experience negative feelings.

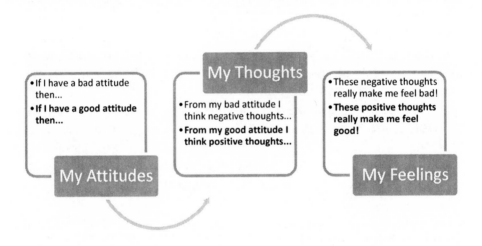

The key is to harness a good attitude most of the time, if not all of the time!

EXERCISE EIGHT

In this last exercise, you are going to trace the trajectory of your negative feelings by not only getting to the root of your negative thinking, but also the negative attitudes that underlie them. These negative attitudes might have been created ages ago, and now is the time to undercover them! The goal here is to start uncovering as many negative feelings as possible and find out where the negative attitude developed. This is not digging too deep or too intensely in the past; rather, it's identifying the attitude for what it is, where it came from, and showing yourself that a past attitude has no relevance in the present moment. When you use attitudes from the past, you are basically stereotyping your present life!

Here is an example of this process I want you to try using to overcome negative attitudes and create positive present moment attitudes:

| COMMON NEGATIVE FEELING (DEPRESSED) | • "I feel depressed and down on myself alot because the same things happen to me over and over again."
 • "No matter how hard I try to feel good about myself, I still feel down!" |

| MY THOUGHT THAT CREATES THIS FEELING (I AM NOT WORTHY) | • "Everybody else always gets the breaks and not me. I am a loser?"
 • "Life is not fair, it is a crap shoot. The lucky ones get all of the opportunities!" |

| ATTITUDE (NEGATIVE)I AM A VICTIM, BAD THINGS ALWAYS HAPPEN TO ME! | • "Your life is what it is and you have to take what you get!"
 • "There is no sense in trying, I was born on the wrong side of the tracks to the wrong family and have a disadvantage!" |

NEGATIVE ATTITUDE PROGRESSION

Okay, you see how you can trace your feelings backwards to get the thoughts you are using to create the feelings? It is very simple. You act like a detective to get at your thoughts as your feelings are readily available – probably the most intense aspect of your awareness. Now the more challenging part of this exercise is getting at your attitude from stripping away your thoughts. Remember, the longer your attitudes crystallize, the more readily, stereotypical your thoughts become. Change your attitudes and you change your thoughts and then your feelings will resonate positively and joyfully! Here is a positive version of this same exercise whereby positive feelings are traced backwards:

POSITIVE ATTITUDE PROGESSION

Okay, see how you can get to the root of your feelings and thoughts by zoning in on your attitudes? Now it is your turn to try this! Try this exercise daily for 30 days. Uncover the negative attitudes that are locking your thoughts in a negative mode. Once you are able to uncover the negative attitudes, you are on your way!

NEGATIVE ATTITUDE PATTERNS

MY NEGATVE FEELING IS: _____

- This is how I would describe my most common negative feelings ...

NEGATIVE THOUGHTS CREATING THIS NEGATIVE FEELING: _____

- This is the negative thought pattern I keep using to create this negative feeling...

MY BAD ATTITUDE IS: _____

- Describe in depth the negative beliefs you keep to create this bad attitude you have...

BREAKING DOWN NEGATIVE THINKING

Excellent! Now you are ready to do the reverse! Take each negative feeling, negative thought and negative attitude you have and turn them around until you come up with positive feelings derived from positive thoughts because you have given yourself a positive attitude adjustment! Start with the positive feeling you want and then work toward the thoughts required to create it and then the new attitudes you need to engrain in your mind to establish consistent healthy, positive thoughts and feelings:

POSITIVE ATTITUDE PATTERNS

POSITIVE FEELING I WANT IS: _____

• This feeling would feel like...

POSITIVE THOUGHTS CREATING THE DESIRED FEELING: _____

• If I want to feel the desired feeling, these are the thoughts I just created for myself...

POSITIVE ATTITUDE TO CREATE MY DESIRED POSITIVE THOUGHTS: _____

• My attitude for sparking and creating positive thoughts for myself is...

CREATING POSITIVE THOUGHT PATTERNS

If you are willing and able to work through doing this positive thought progression program for 30 days, you will be a mastermind – THE MASTER OF YOUR MIND controlling all thoughts which lead to all feeling states!

189

CLOSING THOUGHTS:

BRINGING CLOSURE TO YOUR PAST TO HAVE BETTER TODAY'S

"You must live in the present, launch yourself on every wave; find your eternity in each moment. Fools stand on their island opportunities and look toward another land. There is no other land, there is no other life but this."

Henry David Thoreau

I have presented a lot of information in this book. Some of it may sound familiar – stuff you already know. Other information might be "the stuff" that you are hearing for the first time. From the countless clients and individuals with mental health disorders and addictions I have worked with over the years I have learned one thing about applying these principles and methods...they work!

The key to success in life, for anything is two-fold: belief and persistence. You have to believe in yourself. You are capable of doing great things in your life. You deserve a wonderful life; after all, that is why you are on this earth. Believing in others who have gone before you, are capable of helping you, or are concurrently doing what you want to do/become is a tremendous part of the belief principle. Reaching outside of yourself is what many who have found greatness, success, and better lives have done. In the end, they were better off for it!

Persistence will keep you on the journey you want to be on. It will take you where you want to go. There will always be obstacles in life and persistence will help you overcome these inconveniences and set-backs. Any setback is always as "set-up" for overcoming these inconveniences. This helps build character, strength, resilience and the ability to lead not only yourself, but others on life's amazing journey. Persistence will always bring you that much closer to that which you most want in life. Guess what? That which most often is so close to you, within grasping distance but you don't see it yet! And this, my friends, is all about FAITH!

FAITH = BELIEF + PERSISTENCE

Faith encompasses both belief and persistence. When you have both you are a tremendous, powerful potential embarking on and creating success for yourself. Faith is seeing when things are still in the unseen. It is knowing that things will happen, things will show up in your life that you are hoping for...knowing it is all just around the corner, or in your own life already but just below the surface, roots planted deeply with the sprouts about to shoot up toward the Divine light of the sun. Keep the faith you will quickly learn that all things are possible (with God/a Higher Power) and that the life you yearn to live is already here. You just have to ask for it, believe in it and claim it as your own!

I hope that you will find your journey through life positively enriched after reading this book and applying the principles. Any and all change begins and ends with you. What are you waiting for?

 aith is taking the first step even when you can't see the whole staircase.

~ Martin Luther King Jr.

SECTION THREE

USING DAILY INTENTIONS TO OVERCOME ADDICTION, VICES, BAD HABITS AND FOR A NEW WAY OF THINKING POSITIVELY

You are about to embark on a 30 day program of intentional readings (intentions) which will help re-create, reshape and affirm new ways for thinking and perceiving your life. It is best to read these over each morning upon wakening before your mind becomes cluttered with concerns.

I use the concept of "intentions" rather than "affirmations for two reasons: 1) Actively choosing and 2) Powerfully expecting outcomes. When you *ACTIVELY* chose something, you are engaging your mind rather than being a receptacle and allowing things to free flow into it like a garbage can and create clutter. Actively choosing and pursuing means you are engaging, learning and conditioning your mind on your terms. When you *POWERFULLY* expect outcomes, you usually get them through law of attraction and power of expectation. Setting an intention and believing it will come to pass is a powerful expectation and demonstrates strength in one's beliefs, abilities and for the Universe to bring into your life what you believe you will deserve. No disrespect to the concept of "affirmation", but for how many use them is pointless – they do nothing more than read them over or repeat them but never powerfully believe in them. Also, setting an intention places power over it as it "coming to be" a reality, or already claiming it when using it in the past tense, as already coming to be.

I strongly recommend reading these intentions several times a day thus letting the words seep into your unconscious mind. It is also a very good idea to add a positive feeling to the "believing" component, "feeling" each time that you are who you want to be . Enjoy!

> # DAY ONE
> ## I choose to live today feeling empowered, strong and in control of my mind...I am master of my mind!

You are what you think you are! If you believe that you were destined to be a great person, then you can start living that greatness right now as you are truly the master of your own destiny. To many people believe that they are nothing more than puppets on a string or actors on a stage being led around by some crazed director making them do things they do not want to do. Furthermore, some people believe there is a "master mind" (God, the Universal Mind or some deity) which does all of their thinking for them. Wrong! As a human being you have free will which means that you have the freedom to pick and choose your thoughts, feelings and actions. Remember that thoughts create the seeds for feelings that will manifest and these feelings will often determine the way you act. Isn't it a good idea to take control of your mind and choose the thoughts that will make you feel great?

What are you waiting for? Can you feel the change coming over you right now? Doesn't your body feel lighter, but also stronger? That strong sense of vitality, inner strength and "happiness" is all about you because you are "you" and choosing to feel great because you are the master of your thoughts! Today you will remind yourself throughout the day that you are in control of your thoughts at all times, especially those moments when you feel negativity seeping in. You will nip it in the bud immediately and remind yourself saying, "I am empowered, strong and in control of my thoughts and I choose only good, positive healthy thoughts. I am the me that I want to be!"

DAY TWO
Thoughts become things! Since I prefer good feelings I will *choose* positive thoughts because I want my feelings to be great!

Too many people live "by proxy" when it comes to their thoughts in that they just go with the flow, they let their thoughts control them, rather than controlling their thoughts. Thoughts become things – feelings, attitudes and actions. The longer you focus on a thought the more likely its corresponding feeling will manifest in you. Unfortunately many people focus on the thoughts that they don't even want to think about. Sounds kind of crazy right?

You see, people become conditioned to their own thought patterns, even when they are negative. The reason that this happens for so many is that they don't challenge existing thought patterns, even the negative ones because they either just accept them or perhaps are just too lazy to put in the effort. If you are thinking and acting on negative thought patterns, then it is time to fix it! You know the saying, "If it isn't broken, don't fix it?" Guess what? It's broken! If you are continually feeling feelings that are depressing, anxious, angry, sad, vindictive, negative or self-loathing then you know your thought system needs a tune-up and fast!

The best way to tune up your thought system and make it work more efficient and consistently stable, rather than fast and furious is to feed it with "higher octane" high grade thoughts. When you focus on good feelings you instantly create a shift in the mind and cause the cylinders to all kick in and ramp up to a level of higher energy feelings. These feelings that you are creating for yourself have the ability to not only make you feel happier, stronger and confident, but they begin attracting positive situations, experiences and people into your life! Fill'er up with great, positive thoughts!

DAY THREE
I am not my past! I am not what I said, think or did! I am "ME", a free thinker to choose, think, feel and act in this present moment!

There are a lot of people who carry the burdens of their pasts (actions, failures, mistakes, etc.) around with them believing this is their punishment or act of contrition. Some people believe that the longer they hold onto these hardships, the greater reward they will receive "somewhere" and "sometime" down the road. Guess what? That "somewhere" and "sometime" will never come because the more one holds onto their negativity, the more it becomes engrained, encrusted and embedded in them like petrified wood! This negativity becomes a character attribute and difficult to separate from their being. Furthermore, some people actually becomes used to this mental/emotional suffering and identify with it so much it gives them a sense of importance. If that isn't enough, they are often in the presence of others who think the same way. After all, misery loves company!

If you think like this, you will always be waiting for that "day" to come when everything gets better. That "day" is an illusion because it is a moment hoped for but never attained because there is no set time or place, well at least according to the one who thinks this way!

There is a time and place for one to let the burdens of the past go. You might be asking, "Okay, when is that day?" Guess what, it is closer than you think. As a matter of fact, it is right here, right now! The day, that "specific day" you hope for and forecast change will come in your life is what you are living in right now. You control the present moment and all that is in it. And you know those burdens you think you have to carry around with you? Give yourself permission to let them go...yes, right now! The "day" is here and you are ready to live in the present moment shaping a future you hoped for!

DAY FOUR
I will live with a backbone mentality releasing my wishbone attitude!

Too many people live with what I call a wishbone attitude – hoping for the best, but expecting the worst. They "wish, wish and wish" some more but they are always in a "wishing" mode rather than a believing mode which leads to action. Some people really believe that a fairy godmother or genie is going to just show up in their lives and drop into their lap what they've always been wishing for even though they don't want to invest the effort (faith and work) into what they want most. When things do not happen for them, they revert deeper into their wishbone attitude claiming that, "They were dealt a bad hand of cards!", or "Good things happen to everyone else except them!" and they revert to the "Why them and not me?" mentality. Then their "wishers" kick in..."I wish I could be like so and so..." etc. This is a wishbone attitude and will always keep you in a place of wishing and never attaining.

A backbone mentality is one of belief, faith and expectation. People with backbone mentalities believe, "If it is ever going to be, then it is up to me to get whatever it is in motion." Having a backbone mentality means taking the first steps or starting action on a dream to get momentum on your side. In truth, wishbones break easy because they are split. Backbones are pliable but strong because they support the entire structure. So what is holding you "back" from having a backbone mentality? As Larry the Cable Guy would say, "Git-R-Done!"

DAY FIVE
Happiness is a decision and choice only I can make for myself. Today I choose to feel happy!

Many people believe with the misconception that someone or something outside of them self is responsible for their happiness. In fact, this is perhaps one of the most deceiving bill of goods ever bought by individuals who subscribe to this mentality! They believe that they have to be rich, own certain products, be popular, have everyone like them, or have their dream career to be happy. This is totally not true. As a matter of fact, many people have all of these things or acquire them one by one and they are still not happy. Why is that? After all, they have everything they thought that would make them happy...

You see, happiness cannot be bought, and in fact, it can't even be taught! Only you can think, feel, act and eventually become happy. You are the only one who can recognize and know what true happiness means to you. Best of all it starts and finishes with you because it is internal. You don't have to wait for someone else or something outside of you to make you happy as you have all of the ingredients needed to make you "yourself" happy. The most important anyone can ask you, including yourself is, "What are you waiting for?" The choice is your own to think and feel whatever it is you want. Make a conscious decision moving forward to think happy thoughts and engrain this truth into your mind, "Only I can make myself happy!"

DAY SIX
It's who I truly am inside that really matters most to me!

Who are you? So many people go through life trying to please others. Interestingly, when you try to please others (which is mostly impossible to do all of the time and most of the time) you are more likely to feel like a failure because you can't seem to always keep them impressed by you or happy with you. Often times the harder you try to impress, the harder you fail because you have placed so much emphasis on trying to get other people's approval.

it is not uncommon for people to lose sight of who they really are. They have identified with others for so long as, someone's "significant other", their "other half" or someone's "kid", that their own identify got enmeshed or lost in another's that they truly do not know whom they are. Furthermore, when they feel alone or are alone for the first time and introspect into who and what they are, they feel lost, lonely and scared. They never established an identity for them self because they were always a pleaser about "impressing" someone else. Today, you will only have to impress yourself and this will be easy. Also you need to achieve this missions is the following: 1) Accept yourself unconditionally, 2) Create your own happiness, 3) Know it is okay to make mistakes, and 4) Love yourself with your whole heart and soul!

DAY SEVEN
Today I will choose to live a life of abundance! I am worthy of all the Universe has for me.

The law of attraction asserts that there is enough of everything to go around for everyone. The law of attraction knows no lack, rather "abundance". Since you are a part of an infinite and abundant universe, you are entitled to your share of "more than enough to go around for everyone"!

In order to attract into your life what you most want to receive, you first have to know what it is that you want. Write out your intention, "I intend to attract into my life _____ by this time period _____." Then release your intention in full faith believing that you will attract into your life that what it is that you want most. You will draw into your life only after you are able to let go of it!

The key element is believing that you deserve to have what you want. Up to this point in your life you may have believed that you don't deserve the things you want most because of mistakes you have made in the past. You now know that the past is the past and you are not your past. Therefore, get your mind in an expecting mode as you are indeed deserving!

DAY EIGHT
I have total control over how I react to other people and situations. I am rarely if ever easily offended!

This intention is all based on attitude – your own! No matter what others say to you, talk behind your back, or situations that turn out the way you want them to, you will stay in control over how you react. Moreover, you will act and react calmly and assertively, remaining in total control of your thoughts and feelings at all times.

There will be times and occasions that you feel you were treated unfairly or things just don't make sense. These thoughts leading to any negative feelings will be your cue to remove yourself from the situation and change your focus onto something good. Remember, you are in control of your thoughts at all times even in challenging situations where you feel like you are losing control. As a matter of fact, the feeling of "losing control" is a reminder that you are in total control. This is your moment to tip the balance in your favor for generating positive thoughts and creating uplifting feelings. Remember that the situation itself has a minimal effect on you and it is your reaction to the situation that has the more profound effect. Therefore, choose to act positive!

DAY NINE

I am empowered! The victim's mentality that I may have had in the past no longer holds any part in the way I think today!

You will only be as strong as you think you are! Feeling and being empowered is a mindset that you create for yourself. Many people who have addictions and mental health issues feel like they were victimized by the wrong doings of others or by the circumstances they faced in the past. That is fine and dandy because that was the past and that was a "past" perception you might have held.

Today you are someone who has overcome their past, and the struggles associated with the past. You are ready, willing and able to move ahead with possibility thinking which is based on feeling empowered – you can do all things that you set your mind to. With the help of God/the Universal Mind, you are able to transcend weak and limited thinking and stretch the boundaries of possibilities for believing and achieving. Make your dreams and goals big enough for God/the Universal Mind to fit in!

DAY TEN
Today I realize I am right where I need to be at this moment in time. All is unfolding perfectly with the right timing!

You are where you need to be in this given moment in time. There is a saying, "When the student is ready, the teacher will appear!" Too many people try to rush or force their life to unfold immediately. You are definitely the architect to your life and the author of the choices that you make, but sometimes things have to unfold at the "right" pace because timing is everything. You might be ready but people, circumstances and situations might not be ready yet. Synchronicity is everything for the situation to be what is was meant to be. I am a firm believer in the notion that "If it is going to be then it is up to me!" What I believe and buy into this statement most is that your present life is up to you in how your choose to think, feel and act in making choices. You can't control others, but you can control you knowing that you are where you need to be in the moment as this moment is a building block for better and bigger future moments.

DAY ELEVEN
I do not need to understand the "why's" of everything whether they be good or bad. I will just acknowledge the "what's"!

Too many people go through life always needing answers for everything, sometimes even the good things. Their statements often start with the word "Why" and the tone of their statement carries with it a blaming or accusatory overtone. When you always want to know "why's" or demand to know them, you are looking for precise, concise, definitive answers. Guess what? Some people, places or things do not possess an answer to your "why" given their nature. Digging deeper into finding the "why's" will most likely lead you to further frustration and resentment.

When putting "Why" at the start of a sentence, sometimes it is a sign of perfectionism – you not only expect others to be perfect, but often times you see yourself in others which would mean that perhaps you are a perfectionist. Remember, it is all about attitude! Who cares about the "Why?" It is more about how you are going to respond positively.

DAY TWELVE
The me I choose to see is the me that I will be! Today, I will choose to see the best version of me!

Too many people choose to see themselves the way others see them, or how they have always chosen to see themselves based on the past. Often times, the way they came to know and perceive themselves is based on past failures, shortcomings and how others have stereotyped or judged them. Who do you really want to be? Do you want to be someone who is positive and full of possibilities? Do you want to be in control of your own present moment leading to a better future?

Imagine today that you are an artist who has been given a blank canvas and every color of paint that you can possibly imagine. The canvas is a representation of you and the colors are all the qualities and characteristics of the personality you want to create for yourself. Notice that this isn't a "paint by numbers" or "paint in the lines" exercise – this would mean you are constrained by limits. This exercise is intended to make you a no limits possibility thinker. You are encouraged to use any and every color you like and paint the masterpiece, "YOU" who you want to be. The "YOU" that you choose to see will be the "YOU" that you can and will become! What are you waiting for? Use your imagination! Paint something of yourself beyond a Picasso or Monet instead of a "paint by numbers" book! The only constraint that exists here is whatever you choose and the best choice is being constraint-free!

DAY THIRTEEN

The problems or obstacles that I encounter are only as big as I make them. Today I will minimize them and choose to see them as challenges to conquer!

Too many people make their problems or circumstances mountains when they are really molehills! Sure, everyone will have or experience problems. They may not appear fun at all but guess what? Problems mean that you are alive and able to function and exert some degree of control over the present moment. In fact, the problem you are encountering might be a crossroad in your life symbolizing that change needs to be made, or that you are experiencing personal growth.

Problems come in all shapes and sizes, and they come at any time! The key to perceiving and/or experiencing your problem is to ask yourself, "Am I bigger than my problem, or is my problem bigger than me?" Remember, you are a part of a Universal Mind/God with infinite potential and possibilities. Many people are quick to stereotype immediate problems based on past experiences, or on current "feeling" states. The key is to get your mind out of the gutter (problem) and into clean air (a calm, cool and collected mind). Sure your problems may not go away over night, may take some time, or some may be permanent.

The goal then is to make them manageable and to become a better person because of them!

DAY FOURTEEN
I will have the courage to make mistakes and learn from them! I will use them as life lessons!

Many people are extremely hard on themselves when they make mistakes. The reason is they view their mistakes as indicative of their self-worth. Perhaps as a child your were punished, degraded or devalued whenever you made a mistake. It was not your fault that you were treated that way, instead it was those treating you that way that were wrong. Even though they wronged you, you will not choose to think or act like a victim because of it. Furthermore, you will now move beyond the mentality that, "Whenever I make a mistake or screw up it is a reflection of my self-worth!" This is wrong, stinking thinking and no longer holds a place in the way that you choose to think!

From this day forward view yourself as a curious person, even courageous each time you make a mistake. The reason that you can think and feel this way is because you did something others might not have done...you took a chance! The more changes you take and do things in life, the more mistakes you will make due to two things; you are only human and the law of probability. So embrace being human and taking chances. After all, mistakes are lessons for how to do something better and more efficiently!

DAY FIFTEEN
Today I will learn to live one step at a time, one moment at a time and most importantly, one day at a time!

Have you ever heard of the funny saying, "How do you eat an elephant?" You know the one that answers, "One bite at a time." Of course the moral of the story about eating elephants is not that they taste good or that you should try eating one! The is a metaphor for the way on how to live your life more effectively, successfully and happily.

To many people try to live their entire in one single day! They try to do too much or make lasting changes in one moment which have taken lifetimes to get too or lifetimes to build. The best things in life take time to develop and in essence, "Rome was not built in a day!" People become tired of the way they've been or the way things are and become desperate. This desperation leads to wanting instant change. When that change doesn't come as fast as they like, or they fail at what they are trying to do, they become frustrated, stressed and even depressed. Of course they were not likely to succeed in a single leap – you can't create lasting and intense change in a hastened, short period of time. You have to build on it. Unfortunately, some want change so fast and when it doesn't come yet "again" they spiral. You have to remember that change comes gradually and becomes solidified, fortified and integral over time, but you have to persist with the change you want to become. When you look at the big picture it can be intimidating and overwhelming, so eat your elephant (the changes you want to see) one bite at a time. When you live one day at a time intentionally, you are creating the lasting change you want for yourself!

DAY SIXTEEN
Today I will learn to enjoy and engage my life rather than endure it!

Are you one of those people who dreads getting up in the morning? When you open your eyes do you say, "Oh no, here we go again, I hope today is better than yesterday!"? Do you go through the day reminding yourself that it will end soon and the day will be done with? How about this...no matter which day other than "Friday", are you one that can't wait for Friday to arrive and fast enough? As if Friday is going to possess all of the magical qualities and pixie dust to take you away to some place where there is no stress – dream on! The bottom line: Life is life, it happens for all who are living, it keeps going forward, and you possess the gift of having one, now what are you going to do with it?

Life was meant to be engaged in and enjoyed to the max! Life is not a spectator sport and conversely it is not a gladiator sport – all blood, sweat and tears! Life is about enjoying and appreciating not only the finer moments, but all moments. To truly live means enjoying your life everyday and the people, places and things in them. Today, develop and attitude of gratitude for life. Wake up being thankful that you are alive, for your family, your friends, your job, your health, the comforts and securities of life you possess,

222

etc. Each time you find something to be thankful for, more things will come into your life to be thankful for because you are enjoying life!

DAY SEVENTEEN
I will learn to forgive the wrongs done to me by others. Forgiving does not condone what they did nor does it mean embracing them!

The key to this intention is letting go! Too many people develop hardened hearts and mindsets because they hold onto to wrongs done to them. Furthermore, some people live with the notion that if they truly forgive someone then they are accepting what the person did to them as well as what that person stands for. Wrong!

Forgiveness is done for you, really! It is what you get out of it meaning, emotional, mental and spiritual release. When you hold onto anger and bitterness, it is like drinking poison and waiting for the other person to drop dead. When this negative mindset continues, you are literally taking a new serving of poison daily (poison thinking) and poisoning your mind. When you forgive someone, it is for you to move on and feel good about you!

DAY EIGHTEEN
Today I will remind myself that it is never too late to be the person I want to be. Life is a continual journey and not a destination!

Are you someone who believes that they always need to be "somewhere" in life or have a certain level of success that defines you? If so, you will always be chasing after something that is elusive because the parameters for that measure are never accurately defined and they are constantly changing. You see, live is always changing – you continue to evolve and mature through learning and experiences. With that said, how or what you may have defined yourself to be in terms of success will change because new things come into your life moment by moment, and often times those "things" are thoughts, thoughts that nag you: "I should be a better person!", "I should have this level of financial success in my life!", "I should be happily married!", etc. When you start to get into this "Should be at.." mentality when thinking about what makes you a success, you will be frustrated, helpless and even become desperate. Success is not measured by what you have or accomplished, but it is all about living in the moment and appreciating the moment. That is what successful living is all about...a continual journey!

DAY NINETEEN
I will not procrastinate! I will make things happen today and be the change I want. If it is going to be, then it is all on me!

Too many people treat life like a spectator sport or a wedding to a fancy event – they are waiting for an invitation to come their way! The reality is that life is not a dress rehearsal, it is the real day meaning no mulligan's for time lost. Once that time is gone you can't get it back. Even though the clocks may go back and forth in the Fall and Spring seasons for Daylight Savings Time, you can never "save" time.

Today you want to develop a mindset that you are able, willing and eager to jump into things...your life! Do whatever it is you are putting off. Once you start things, you gain momentum and the proverbial ball starts to roll. Sometimes the hardest part is just getting started and once you do and start to succeed, you wonder why the heck you waited so long! Fret not, no time for regrets or second thoughts because your mind is in the game and you are rolling forward!

DAY TWENTY
Today I will accept and live with the understanding that all great things come to those who believe! I will believe in me!

You will never reach or achieve goals in life at the level you want if you don't believe in you...simple! Achievement is all based on faith and belief in one's true self. People outside of you can encourage you and this might motivate you, but it all starts with your own beliefs, especially the one that you have about you – you can accomplish anything you put your mind to!

Some people argue that there are those "born with silver spoons" in their pockets who have rich parents, or get the breaks. They believe "these breaks" or families lead to their accomplishments, maybe in some cases, but what about the others? You know, the throngs of kids/teens and adults who are wealthy and come from good families who wind up in rehab or miserable? And what about those who come from slums, poverty and abuse and rise to the occasion making great successes of themselves? The different is "BELIEF"! If you want to achieve and be all that you are intended to be, then you have to believe you can!

DAY TWENTY-ONE
I can and I will! Today I will live like I have already been to where I want to be!

If you go where you want to in the mind, really "feeling" the sensations for how the experience will be when you really get there, you will get there! The energy that you will create will pull to you the experiences you imagine and feel inside your mind. Do you think it is a coincidence you are drawn to certain people, places or things? No! Do you think it is random chance the same types of negative situations or dysfunctional people keep showing up in your life? No!

Today you will feel who and what you want to be or go to in your mind. Spend 10-20 minutes meditating and truly getting into this feeling state. Of course focus on the positives you want to happen. Before you know it, the energy you are sending out will bring back to you similar experiences!

DAY TWENTY-TWO
Today I will be open- minded to greater possibilities. Just because I don't understand something doesn't make it bad or wrong. I will listen attentively!

Many people judge others before knowing the facts, or say "no" to someone or something before even considering it. Lazy and stereotypical thinking is at the root of this and until you overcome this and take the blinders and rose-colored glasses off, you will never see the "big picture"!

Too many people "get stuck" where they are because they literally think inside of the box – the box they created for themselves. This box is complete with stereotypes, judgments, criticisms, and knee jerk decisions based on prior experiences. Instead of trying something new by "thinking something new", they revert to their conditioned and limited thinking pattern. Have you ever wondered why some things are always the same?

Your goal today is to catch yourself whenever you are about to make a knee-jerks response before thinking things through. Today, you will listen attentively and empathize with that others are saying. Once you engage this skill and practice it, you will find that your mind will open to greater possibilities and these greater possibilities will chase you down!

DAY TWENTY-THREE
I have the courage to trust others! In sharing my secrets with others I prove to myself that I have the ability to trust others as well as myself!

Anyone who has had an addiction or mental health issue they have dealt with has probably struggled with trust issues. Who can you trust, right? Actually, can you even trust your own judgments and choices?

It seems when you get hurt or let down by someone you trust you have a hard time trusting that person again. When it happens again and again, you have difficulty trust people period! Eventually, over time you wonder if you can trust anyone because you start to question your own abilities in being a good judge of character. Today your ability to heal and become a stronger person comes from trusting, both yourself and others.

People are and always will be social creatures and we need others just as they need us. Someone needs you today because they trust you. Likewise, it is okay to trust again because you will need someone. There truly is a circle of trust with you being in and of that circle!

DAY TWENTY-FOUR
Today the only person I want to be better than is the one that I was yesterday. This is a sign of my personal growth!

Too many people wish they were someone else or someone different. First off, if you were someone different, you would just inherit a different set of problems, perhaps more! You would then probably wish you were someone else again, perhaps yourself again?

Second, if you really want to be someone different, then be someone different, a better version of you! This intention today shows that you have the power to change whom and what you want to be based on your perception of self. You can definitely be "that person" you want to be by being a better version of yourself!

Today, make it your intention to do, try and be better than you were yesterday. Believe in yourself knowing that you were meant to live a life of integrity.

DAY TWENTY-FIVE
Today I will choose to live with options. The only walls that exist in my life are the ones that I create!

There are so many people who believe that they are trapped or held up in corners because they have no options. Some believe that life is life a prison where they are forced to do the same thing day in and day out. Life for them is nothing more than a routine!

If you are living, breathing and have any form of health, and free, then life is not a prison, rather a gift and privilege to enjoy and embark on daily. The only reason prison is the one you live in between your ears. Recall Viktor Frankl who was a real prisoner in a Nazi death camp. Even he believe he was a free man in his head and how he chose to perceive things.

You may possess an addiction or mental illness, but that doesn't make you a prisoner or helpless to it. You are free to move beyond where you think you are at and transcend to a new level today. So do it!

DAY TWENTY-SIX
Today I will choose to permanently live free of labels/stereotypes and be the person who I know that I truly am inside me others may not know!

You are not your addiction! You are not your mental health illness! You are not your bad habits or your vices! And you are not a "bad" person!

Too many people live with the label they have been given and identify with it. They embrace and use the negative connotation they have been given and take it on with their name or actually make it their name. You are more than the characteristics you posses whether they are good or bad!

You are a complete individual with an infinite spirit! To take on a label and make it a part of you in a negative and self-destructive way undermines your true essence as well as what you Creator intended for you. Today you will tell yourself that you are a complete person, made perfectly, fully loaded with potential and ready to strive for new levels of life and happiness. No label should ever keep you from your life's destination or happiness. You are more and better than any labels!

DAY TWENTY-SEVEN
I am happy! I choose happiness for myself. I am a happy person!

Many people wait for happiness to find them or chase them down. Others are always looking for happiness. Moreover, many never find happiness nor will they ever! Is happiness some sort of special quality only given to a select few? Herein lies the problem...happiness is not given, it is accepted!

The only person who can make you happy is you. You have everything right here and right now to make yourself happy. It all starts with the mindset and choice – *I choose to be happy!*

There is nothing magical about happiness, no! The only thing magical about happiness is that when you apply it and choose to be it, you feel "happy" and life around you feels more "magical"!

DAY TWENTY-EIGHT
I am great! I will think highly of myself because I owe it to myself!

Today's intention focuses on greatest – your greatness! There is nothing wrong with feeling and thinking you are great. After all, if you want to go great things in life, you need the attributes of greatness.

Thinking that you are "great" does not mean that you go around life with an inflated ego and think that you are better than anyone else. Remember, throughout the course of this book, you are no longer comparing yourself to other people, only to whom and what you were the day before. You are striving to become a better person each day, full of dignity and integrity. You are also thinking "great" thoughts that are filled with possibility, potential and are positive. To think great, you have to be great, not average, mediocre or all right! You have the right to think, feel and be great. You don't have to wait for anyone's permission to think this way. If you think this way, then basically, you are in a feeling "less than others" position and ironically, you perceive them as being "greater than you"! To heck with that mentality! Choose the greatness you want to be and right now for you are not a door mat or less than anyone else, and not less than who you think you are!

DAY TWENTY-NINE
Today I am aware that the changes I am making in my life are continual steps to greater and lasting change!

Everything that you have learned in this book and continue to learn from this book and from other positive sources will be continual stepping stones for lasting change in your life. See your life not only as a journey but a wonderful process that gets better and better each day.

Many people want change now. Guess what? You are getting your wish as change is happening in the present moment if you are thinking and believing it is happening. With that said, the results of the change may take some time to manifest, but they are developing and you only need to believe that it is happening. Two years, five years, or 10 years from now you can look back and really see how far you have come – growing in a positive direction!

DAY THIRTY
Right now I am self-empowered possessing complete control over my life and the choices I make for the life I want!

This book is all about self-efficacy – teaching you how to develop confidence, greater awareness and self-esteem so you can complete whatever goals and tasks that you set your mind to. The decision to believe that you can achieve your goals rests solely on your shoulders. In the past you may have believed you were a victim of circumstances, that life was unfair, or that good things only came to "good" people.

Now that you have read this book, you know that not only are you "great" but you are entitled to choose the life you want to lead because you have SELF-EFFICACY. You my friend are FREE! You have the knowledge to be whatever you want to be and get to wherever you want in life. There are no more excuses, there are only choices. This is the best part of being FREE and having SELF-EFFICACY!

REFERENCES

Bandura, A. (1960). Relationships of family patterns to child behavior disorders (Progress report, USPHS, Project No. M-1734). Stanford, CA: Stanford University.

Beck, A.T. (1976). Cognitive therapy and emotional disorders. New York: Internations Universities Press.

Beck, A.T. (1991). Cognitive Therapy. American Psychologist, 46, 368-375.

Berne, E. (1964). Games people play. New York: Grove Press.

Diagnostic and Statistical Manual of Mental Disorders, Fourth Edition (DSM-IV) American Psychological Association 1994.

Ellis, E. (2004). The Road to Tolerance: The Philosophy of Rational Emotive Behavior Therapy. Prometheus Books.

Frankl, V. (1997). Man's Search For Meaning. Pocket Books; Rev Upd edition

Freud, S. (1943). A general introduction to psychoanalysis. Garden City, NY; Garden City Publishing. (Originally published 1971).

Maslow, A.H. (1968). Towards a psychology of being (2nd ed.). Princeton NJ: Van Nostrand.

Rogers, C. (1980). A Way of Being. Mariner Books.

Sacco, P. (2007). What's Your Anger Type? Inkstone Press; Australia.

Schuller, R. H. (1985). The Be Happy Attitudes. W. Publishing Group.
Weiten, W. (2011). Psychology: Themes and Variations. Wadsworth

Want to learn more about your anger and ways to manage it better? Read Peter's latest book What's Your Anger Type?